COVENTRY PATMORE'S ANGEL

I Presume
H. M. Stanley's Triumph and Disaster
(Bles, 1956, 1973, New English Library paperback, 1974,
Alan Sutton paperback, 1988)

The Knight and the Umbrella
An account of the Eglinton Tournament
(Bles, 1963, Alan Sutton paperback, 1986)

The Scandal of the Andover Workhouse
(Bles, 1973, Alan Sutton paperback, 1984)

Oscar Browning
A Biography
(John Murray, 1983)

COVENTRY PATMORE'S ANGEL

A study of
Coventry Patmore,
his wife Emily and
The Angel in the House
by

IAN ANSTRUTHER

HAGGERSTON PRESS

Typeset by Fakenham Photosetting Ltd,
Fakenham, Norfolk
Printed in Great Britain
by Redwood Press Ltd, Melksham

1 869812 08 5

Contents

Illustrations

Illustration Acknowledgements

I thank the following for permission to include the pictures in this book: 1 (ownership untraced); 2 (the Author); 3, 5 Barbara Rennie; 6, 7 Guildhall Library, Corporation of London; 8 Julia Bastian; 9 (ownership untraced); 4, 10, 12 Mary Patmore; 11 Jenny Young; 13 London Borough of Camden, Local Studies Library; 16 National Portrait Gallery; 15 Mrs Eva Reichmann and the Tate Gallery.

For Harriet

Introduction

OVENTRY PATMORE'S poem *The Angel in the House*, the
first part of which was written in 1854, was published for
the last time as a work on its own in the summer of 1923,
the centenary year of his birth.[1] An exhibition of its first and
other editions was held at the London Library, under the super-
vision of Edmund Gosse who owned the manuscript; all the
important periodicals contained references to it; the *Daily Telegraph* even sent Arthur Waugh, Evelyn Waugh's father, on a
literary pilgrimage to the site of Patmore's cottage in which he
claimed, incorrectly, that Patmore had written the poem.
Waugh wrote in his column,[2]

As I stood this morning on the edge of the little garden at North-End,
Hampstead, where he dreamed and wrote 'The Angel in the House',
the prevailing sentiment in my heart was one of grateful certainty that,
however varied and depressing the vicissitudes of literary fame, the
quality of true genius will always come into its own at last. For surely,
among that small company whose choice in literature counts for anything, Coventry Patmore's reputation never stood higher than it does
today . . . the best of his poetry is among the very best of its generation.
It is even more than that; it has its place in the intimate sanctuary of
English verse, at the very foot of the altar.

The popularity of *The Angel in the House* had been immense. It
had appeared in more than twenty editions during Patmore's
lifetime. Its title, as a phrase, had become ubiquitous, put to use
to describe not only womanly perfection, but even that of pets.
'*A Dog Day*' or '*The Angel in the House*' by Walter Emanuel,
pictured by Cecil Aldin and dedicated to W. W. Jacobs, had
come out in 1902; the first of many such uses to characterise
ironically or otherwise, the so-called heavenly behaviour of any
living creature within a domestic establishment.

In its day, understandably, it threatened a whole generation of young women before their liberation became an established fact in the twentieth century. Virginia Woolf wrote in *The Death of the Moth*, published in 1942[3]

In those days, the last of Queen Victoria, every house had its Angel. I will describe her as shortly as I can. She was intensely sympathetic. She was immensely charming. She was utterly unselfish. She excelled in the difficult arts of family life. She sacrificed herself daily. If there was chicken, she took the leg; if there was a draught, she sat in it – in short she was so constituted that she never had a mind or a wish of her own, but preferred to sympathize always with the minds and wishes of others. Above all – I need not say it – she was pure. Her purity was supposed to be her chief beauty – her blushes, her great grace. It was she who bothered me and wasted my time and so tormented me that at last I killed her. It is far harder to kill a phantom than a reality. She was always creeping back when I thought I had despatched her. Though I flatter myself that I killed her in the end, the struggle was severe.

Virginia Woolf's killing of the Angel in her own mind must have been only one of many such murders. Arthur Waugh's vision of the poem's immortality has not materialised. Today, nearly one hundred years after Patmore's death, few members of the general public have heard of *The Angel in the House*, and fewer still have read it. However, the poem has been analysed by scholars in recent years for what it reveals of Patmore's views on love and marriage. As Peter Gay has written in his book *The Tender Passion*, it has been 'remorselessly scanned for its exemplification of bourgeois sexual myths and their psychological roots.'[4] I have not attempted to cover this ground again. Instead, I have tried to do what has not been done before: to follow the publication of the book itself, its failure and success and the unexpected adoption of its title in late-Victorian times as a catch-phrase to describe the model wife in a way that had scarcely any connection with the contents of the poem.

Inevitably, however, other themes have crept into the story. Family backgrounds, so vital and fascinating, and largely unresearched, have come to form part of this work. On the other hand, many important aspects of Coventry's life, especially his religious development, his agnosticism in youth and conversion to Rome in maturity, are mentioned only in passing. His biographer, Basil Champneys, has written about all this at length and there is no point in doing so again.

My objective has been simply to write something new about Coventry and Emily Patmore, and about the history of the poem to which their names are linked. My hope is that those who already know *The Angel in the House*, and who know, too, a little about the lives of the Pre-Raphaelites and others who were the first to read it, will enjoy this study. The poem's fate was unexpected, and far removed from Coventry's dreams or those of his wife, his Emily, his 'angel', for whom he proudly wrote it. If Patmore had called his poem something else, its history might have been different. He had planned at first to call it *The Happy Wedding*, and why he changed his mind is not recorded. The title he chose was not original, having been used by Leigh Hunt twenty years earlier for a fourteen-line poem of no merit. Hunt's poem sank without trace, and Patmore's composition might have done the same under another title; for as a work it was banal and not popular when it came out. In May, 1848, Patmore wrote an article on Tennyson's *The Princess* for the *North British Review*. In it he said, 'Poets have often gained their popularity by qualities which must have been regarded by themselves as accidents rather than the essence of their productions.' Nothing he ever penned was more true than this. Although he lived for another forty-eight years, it proved, indeed, to be his own epitaph.

CHAPTER ONE

The Background. The Paradox

T HE YEAR 1862, the twenty-fifth in the reign of Queen Victoria, was one of sorrow in many communities, a year of widespread mourning. To begin with, the nation mourned for Albert, Queen Victoria's cherished spouse, who had died suddenly the previous December; a loss not only for the Royal Family but also one for the whole country. Then there was loss of life in the mines, two hundred men together, when a seam was blocked by falling machinery at Hartley Colliery near Newcastle, and the victims lay entombed for a week. The Queen sent a personal message of sympathy. Fifty lives were lost at sea when the *Mars* sank in the Bristol Channel. Twenty-eight were killed by a boiler which burst at a foundry in Staffordshire. Twenty-three were lost in a workhouse at Brownlow Hill, on the edge of Liverpool, when fire engulfed the northern dormitory and trapped the sleeping female inmates, most of whom were little children. Fifteen died and hundreds were hurt when two trains collided near Edinburgh, the most serious passenger accident in Scottish transport history. Hunger also took its toll when the war between the American States stopped the supply of cotton to Lancashire and caused the closure of hundreds of factories. Half a million were unemployed. Without a massive charitable effort, nearly all of them might have died. Deaths recorded in that year exceeded those in the one before. With characteristic understatement the Registrar General pronounced the statistic 'less than "moderately good"'.[1]

Among Establishment figures, the Archbishop of Canterbury died, the venerable John Bird Sumner; and Admiral Ross, the polar explorer. The Royal Society lost its President, the eminent surgeon Sir Benjamin Brodie. Politics lost John Ricardo, the Free Trader and shipping reformer; the Government mourned for Lord Canning, the outstanding Governor-General of India. Two who had died the previous year were still widely regretted. The sporting world had lost Lord Eglinton, to the deep sorrow of many a knight – the golden youth of the 1830s – who had taken part in his famous tournament in 1839. The literary world had lost an idol, Elizabeth the wife of the poet Robert Browning, whose run-away marriage and tender poetry had thrilled all hearts. Another woman who died, Emily Augusta Andrews, the wife of the poett, Coventry Patmore, remained unmourned except by her family and in her husband's literary coterie. Yet her image, and what she came to stand for – the loving, docile, prudent wife – was to cast a spell on a generation. She was nothing more and nothing less than the Angel in the House.

Coventry's struggle to write his poem, and the way in which it affected his life, provides a fascinating literary study. He and Emily were both poor; both the children of bankrupt parents; both determined to make their home a real haven of peace and security. Emily did so very successfully. Their house became a meeting place for many aspiring writers and painters, especially amongst the Pre-Raphaelite Brotherhood, as well as for stars in the world of letters like Tennyson, Ruskin and Carlyle. She managed the household very efficiently. She bore and cared for six children. She even wrote a domestic manual for the benefit of inexperienced servants, which still remains of genuine interest. Coventry's contribution was literary. He worked by day in the British Museum as one of several assistant librarians; at home he wrote reviews and articles to augment his extremely meagre salary. His real work, however, was verse, and for Emily he wrote the famous poem with which her name became associated, an intellectual dissertation in four books, in a homely metre woven round a conventional romance, in praise of love and domestic happiness.

He believed it would be a real success since those of his friends who were poets themselves and who read it before it reached the bookshops, praised its theme and technical skill, and understood what he meant to convey, that a happy marriage is an earthly foretaste of the love of God to be known in Heaven. In the event, it failed completely. The arrangement was difficult to under-stand, being a series of disjointed 'accompaniments' which con-

stantly broke the flow of the narrative. The story itself was
extremely trite, that of a daughter of the Dean of Salisbury who
lived with her father in 'Sarum Close'. She was wooed and won
by her father's ward, a local squire with a handsome property. Its
few charming, effective passages were swamped by its lack of
originality, damned outright by its simple metre of rhyming
octosyllabic quatrains.

Its failure, after years of work, shattered Coventry's creative
spirit. Then followed Emily's death. His whole world, human
and literary, seemed to have fallen apart at once in a double,
personal disaster. His only hope was complete change. After a
while he married again and, his new wife having money, he gave
up his job in the British Museum, and left London to live in the
country. He joined the Roman Catholic Church, something
Emily had always feared, believing, as an Evangelical, that if he
did she would never see him, once she had taken her place in
heaven. Also, he gave up secular poetry, except for occasional
compositions of which 'The Toys' was the most successful, and
turned his talents to religious mysticism. His former life seemed
forgotten, his old friends unremembered, *The Angel in the House*
a thing of the past, never to be read again.

Years went by; then social changes, borne along by the current
of the times, created a popular use for the poem, and with it, by
an interesting paradox, a place for Emily in history. Ever since
the 1850s when the first societies had formed to support it,
Woman's claim to independence, especially her right to sit in
Parliament, had been voiced with ever increasing energy; her
place in the home as her husband's chattel, challenged with ever
mounting success. On the other hand, there was the man's
viewpoint – widely supported by women, too – that a woman's
place was in the home, creating calm, order and comfort; she was
a priestess in charge of a shrine, at which was laid the daily
offering – the money earned by the striving spouse. This ideal
was upheld with equal determination. Looking to describe this
stereotype in a convenient phrase, society chose 'The Angel in
the House', against whom was ranged 'the Strong-Minded
Woman' of the feminists. The fact that Emily was long dead,
made the selection all the easier. Thus, by chance, she became the

icon of all the lovers of 'Home Sweet Home', the symbol of woman's traditional role.

The effect on the poem, and thus on Coventry, was slow, but quite sensational. The poem began to sell in thousands, especially so in a cheap edition. When it was put together with taste, bound in leather and tooled in gilt, it became an irresistible gift from every innocent, hopeful groom to every unsophisticated bride. It was not always understood, but it looked nice on the drawing-room table. Emily became a literary heroine. Coventry became a domestic figurehead, even though he had married again. They were seen as the archetypal couple, the epitome of all connubial virtue, something both of them would have denied. Coventry rarely spoke of Emily. When he did so it was to reiterate that, while she had been his inspiration, she had never been what the public supposed, the heroine of the book itself. The 'Angel', he said, was the Angel of Love with no specific human counterpart. Nevertheless, in the Family Bible, when he entered Emily's death, he filled it out in the following manner. First he put in the simple facts. '*Died* July 5th 1862 a little before midnight Emily Augusta, wife of Coventry K. D. Patmore, aged 38. Buried in Hendon Churchyard.' Then he inserted an epitaph.[2]

> Faults had she, child of Adam's stem,
> But only Heaven knew of them.

Thus, in her death, he admitted the truth, for the lines came from his own poem. Although, in this, they referred to the heroine, the Dean's daughter of 'Sarum Close', in his own mind they referred to Emily. She was the Angel of Love itself; his Angel in the House.

CHAPTER TWO

Emily's Father, Dr Andrews

EMILY PATMORE, the future 'Angel', was born in 1824, on the morning of the 29th of February, thus becoming a leap-day baby, the fifth daughter and eighth child of Dr and Mrs Edward Andrews. The Andrews family lived in Walworth, then a suburban village on the southern fringe of London. Dr Andrews was a Nonconformist minister, the well-loved pastor of a flock which met in a chapel adjoining his house. In the wider world he was loved by others for his interest in music and philanthropic causes. His name is now forgotten, but because naturally enough, all he did concerned his children, his talents and career deserve attention. No study of the 'Angel' would be complete without a pause to give a backward glance towards her father.

Edward Andrews was born in 1787, **the fifth son and** eleventh child of Mordecai Andrews, a Nonconformist pastor of Coggeshall in Essex, and of his wife, Elizabeth Rutt. The Andrews family claimed descent from Thomas Andrews, an Elizabethan seafaring merchant, an Elder Brother of Trinity House, one of whose sons was the famous prodigy of eloquence and learning, Lancelot, Bishop of Winchester. The latter was Dean of the Chapel Royal, a Privy Councillor for England and Scotland, and first on the list of divines appointed to make the Authorised Version of the Bible in 1611. On the female side, closer in time, a forebear was George Rutt, a London druggist, and his wife, Elizabeth Towill, who married in the 1750s. A daughter of these two became Edward's mother, while a son, John, became a distinguished and successful politician and man of letters, an intimate friend of Henry Crabb Robinson, and father-in-law of Thomas Noon Talfourd.

Thus, through both his parents, Edward Andrews inherited useful worldly connections as well as brains, energy and taste.

Emily Patmore's family

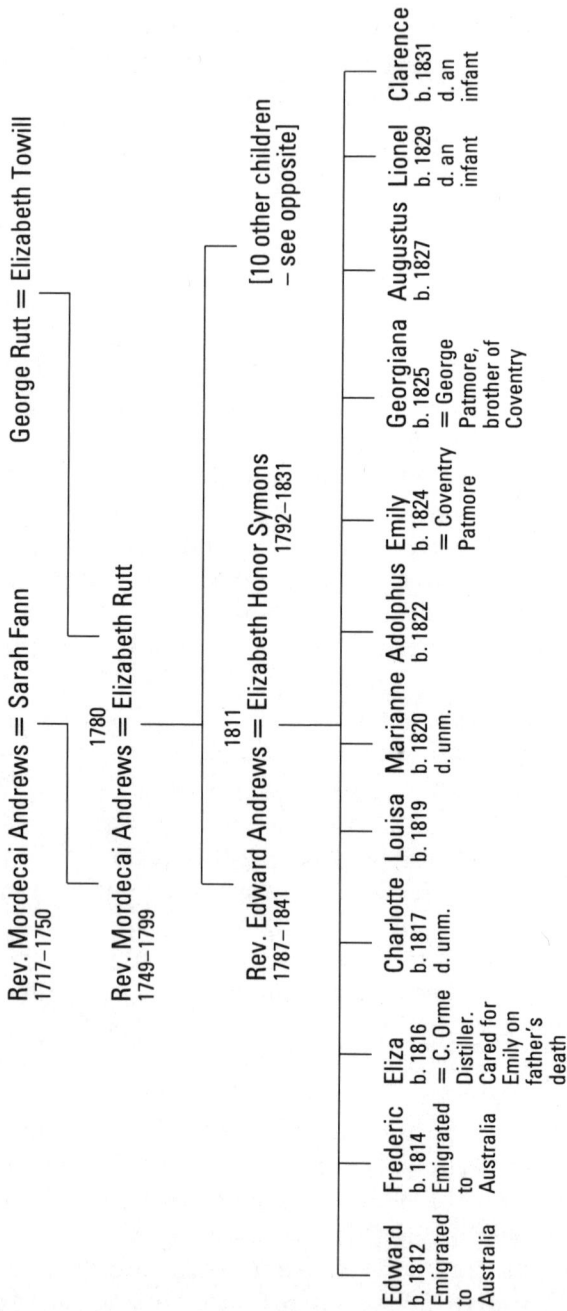

Rev. Mordecai Andrews = Sarah Fann
1717–1750

George Rutt = Elizabeth Towill

1780

Rev. Mordecai Andrews = Elizabeth Rutt
1749–1799

1811

Rev. Edward Andrews = Elizabeth Honor Symons
1787–1841   1792–1831

[10 other children
– see opposite]

Edward	Frederic	Eliza	Charlotte	Louisa	Marianne	Adolphus	Emily	Georgiana	Augustus	Lionel	Clarence
b. 1812	b. 1814	b. 1816	b. 1817	b. 1819	b. 1820	b. 1822	b. 1824	b. 1825	b. 1827	b. 1829	b. 1831
Emigrated to Australia	Emigrated to Australia	= C. Orme Distiller. Cared for Emily on father's death	d. unm.		d. unm.		= Coventry Patmore	= George Patmore, brother of Coventry		d. an infant	d. an infant

Emily Patmore's Uncles and Aunts

Mordecai Andrews = Elizabeth Rutt

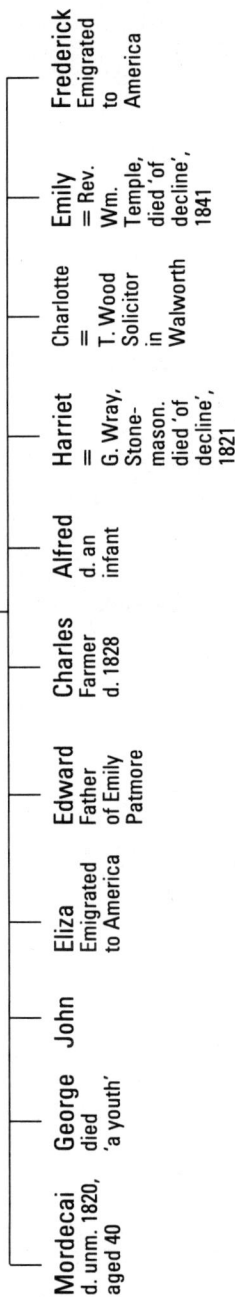

Mordecai d. unm. 1820, aged 40	
George died 'a youth'	
John	
Eliza Emigrated to America	
Edward Father of Emily Patmore	
Charles Farmer d. 1828	
Alfred d. an infant	
Harriet = G. Wray, Stone-mason. died 'of decline', 1821	
Charlotte = T. Wood Solicitor in Walworth	
Emily = Rev. Wm. Temple, died 'of decline', 1841	
Frederick Emigrated to America	

He attended Brown's Academy at Harlow and quickly rose to
the top of the class. This was in 1800. Then family bereavement
struck. His father died and he had to leave school to earn his
living. He exchanged 'pleasant and healthy' Harlow, and Coggeshall's poplars and spreading elms, that legendary seat of rustic
simplicity, for the dirt and noise and bustle of London. He was
set to work in various offices, trying insurance, banking and
commerce, but none of these secured his interest. He decided to
follow his father and grandfather and become a Nonconformist
pastor. In 1798, at the age of twenty-one, he entered Hoxton
Theological College, one of the four religious academies main-
tained for Nonconformist students. Its Principal was famous at
that time, a Scotsman, Dr Robert Simpson, a 'venerable servant
of Christ' as the *Evangelical Magazine* described him.[1] Then
Andrews went to Glasgow University, a common practice
amongst Dissenters, there to study Greek and Logic under pro-
fessors Young and Jardine, both of whom were celebrated
scholars. He left with a coveted 'commendation' for 'propriety,
diligence and eminent abilities.'

He was ordained in 1801 and sent to Romford in Essex, to
comfort the flock in the Bethel Chapel, an imposing, new edifice
in Hornchurch Lane. On being ordained he had also got married,
and here in Romford four children were born: Edward, Frederic,
Eliza, Charlotte. His wife was the daughter of a Cornish car-
penter who had come to London to make his fortune and had
done so quickly, making packing-cases. She was called Elizabeth
Honor Symons, and was born in 1792, thus being nineteen, five
years younger than her husband when they married. They had
met at the famous Surrey Chapel of which the pastor was
Rowland Hill, and across the aisle had fallen in love. Several
years had passed, however, before her parents had agreed to the
marriage.

She was small and fair, with dark eyes which struck everyone
by their beauty. Her daughter Emily was destined to inherit
them. She was fond of music, like her husband, and enjoyed
composing drawing-room songs to which her sisters contributed
the lyrics. One of them still survives in the family. Entitled 'Rosa'
it is hardly a masterpiece, yet has a pleasing simple quality;

Sol's splendid beams dawned o'er the east
The air was fresh one sweet May morn . . .

Her father's wealth was given them freely, both in the service of
God and the family. When, after seven years, her husband's
talents as a fluent preacher began to be known outside Romford,
and to be sought by London congregations, her father built them
a house and chapel in Walworth. Here she gave birth to eight
more children, four boys and four girls, which brought the
family total up to twelve.

The parish of Walworth at that time was still just on the edge
of the country, still the haunt of butterflies and birds, still smell-
ing of hay in the summer and the damp decay of leaves in the
autumn, still, in Pigot's local Directory, only granted the rank of
village or hamlet. It was very swiftly expanding, however, in the
wake of the Industrial Revolution and the rapid increase in the
population. Just a mile and a half from the Thames, directly
south of London Bridge, by the year 1823 its once tranquil
village street had become busy with inns and shops, and the
peaceful lanes which intersected it had been developed with
terraces and villas. East and west were market gardens supplying
London with vegetables and fruit. Immediately south was Camberwell Green, another district soon to be engulfed, beyond
which was Herne Hill and the beautiful woods of Norwood Spa
and Dulwich.

Dr Andrews' chapel and house, of which the chapel still exists,
became known as the Beresford Chapel, being built in Beresford
Street (named after one of Wellington's generals). The street is
now named after John Ruskin because, as a boy, he often went
there. Later on he carefully described the chapel '. . . the Lon-
donian chapel in its perfect type – an oblong, flat-ceiled barn . . .
the pulpit, sublimely isolated . . . and decorated with a cushion of
crimson velvet, padded six inches thick, with gold tassels at the
corners; which was a great resource to me when I was tired of the
sermon, because I liked watching the rich colour of the folds and
creases that came in it when the clergyman thumped it.'[2]

John Ruskin was only a little older than Emily. He greatly
enjoyed her father's sermons, both the preaching and the thump-

ing, and when he got home he wrote them out in tiny notebooks which are still preserved. The only thing he failed to notice or record in any of his later writings was the Beresford Chapel's splendid organ. Built by a well-known manufacturer, George Buckwell of Hackney Road, with 'very superior double diapasons' which gave it a greater range and quality than any other organ in the district, it cost more than a thousand pounds. Many distinguished organists played on it, like Thomas Adams, Samuel Wesley and Benjamin Jacob. They were all Dr Andrews' friends, and they all told him he had been extravagant. He replied that God should be worshipped with the best – the best architecture, the best music and, necessarily, the best instruments. He felt entirely unrepentant. He and his father-in-law had paid for it and had asked for nothing from the congregation. Only his wife complained at times, wanting the money for other purposes. She played, however, as much as he did; and, of course, all the children loved it.

As the Andrews family settled in, they got to know the Ruskins well. At Christmas appropriate gifts were given, and in the summer picnics were arranged in the beautiful country south of Camberwell. The view from Camberwell Grove was superb, a vast panorama of London and the Thames. It made John Ruskin's eyes 'pop out' as he quaintly said one day to his mother. She, a typical worrying mamma, wondered if he was getting sunstroke. Later on, when a little older, he began to admire Emily's sister who lingered with him, picking blackberries, or sang haunting songs of love round the piano in the Andrews' drawing-room. Altogether, they were happy days.

Another delight, closer to home, only a quarter of a mile to the north, was the celebrated Surrey Zoological Garden. Here the children could see giraffes, extremely ferocious lions and tigers, strange monkeys, birds and fishes, as well as amazing ascents in balloons, incredible leaps by Mademoiselle Rossini who flew in the air for three hundred feet; best of all, as dusk fell, terrific eruptions of Mount Vesuvius. Such were the joys of Emily's childhood.

A pastor's life is a very busy one. At all times Andrews was about, either on foot or driving a carriage, hurrying up and down the High Street, gown flying, bands flapping, visiting members of his congregation. Dissenting religion was popular in Walworth, and competition for recruits was keen. In the pulpit his manner was flamboyant, even judged by the standards of a time when dramatics there were quite in order and many of the finest preachers of the day could easily have made their living as actors. He had wonderful gifts of expression and fluency, holding his congregations spellbound, either with tears or smiles or both, as he opened the meanings of complex passages in the simplest conversational terms; frightening those with guilty consciences by awful visions of the agonies of Hell; comforting those who felt they were safe with a catalogue of blissful, heavenly sublimities; warning others of the Whore of Babylon, in other words, the Church of Rome, damning its Jesuitical intrigues. 'Oh horrible mystery of mysteries!' he thundered in a sermon taken from Isaiah, 'Babylon, mother of harlots! sanguinary Rome, we denounce thy triple crown in the name of the Most High God, whose faithful servants thou hast murdered, and whose doctrines thou hast obscured! Ill-fated England, already once more toying with that Dalilah . . .'[3] In cold print his scholarship was often criticised for weakness; in the candle-lit warmth of the Beresford Chapel, to a mostly simple congregation, his words fell on tingling ears like stirring notes from the strident trumpets of angels.

From time to time he had agonising tasks. As one of the pastors approved by the Aldermen of the City of London to attend and console convicted criminals, he had to witness executions. He would go to Newgate, visit the cells, counsel courage, urge repentance, and hold the trembling victims' hands until they were tied, ready for the gallows. He had then to endure the awful moment when the waiting crowd in the street was hushed, the Chaplain gave the signal to proceed by pulling a handkerchief out of his sleeve, the great prison bell tolled, and the corpse hung with head askew until removed by waiting gaolers.

By attending one such execution, he acquired a measure of immortality. In June, 1825, he was asked to visit a man named Probert, sentenced to death for stealing a horse. As Probert prepared to walk to the gallows, and had his arms bound to his sides, his hair which was long, lank and grey rose, slowly, perfectly upright. Andrews watched with a shiver of surprise. Ghastly though the story was, he often told it to his friends afterwards. One of them passed it on to *Notes and Queries*.[4] Some years later, in 1870, it achieved an entry in Brewer's *Dictionary of Phrase and Fable*. It is still there, under 'Hair', as a verified case of the rare phenomenon of human hair standing on end with fright.

Four years later, in 1829, he had to go to the scaffold again with a man called Edward Martelly. The latter had forged a banker's cheque for which, under the existing laws, he received the extreme sentence of death. He was only twenty-one at the time, but he faced his punishment with such courage and with such exemplary spiritual resolve that Andrews felt inspired to write about it. He did so at length in *The Spiritual Times*, a new monthly magazine for those with Calvinistic sympathies. He merely meant to uplift readers as well as to give them a salutary warning, but in so doing, once again, he earned the thanks of future historians. The account he gave was of great interest, for although the procedures, of course, were known, gallows recantations commonplace, and stories of last moments popular and always put in the daily papers, they had never before been described like this in four long monthly instalments by someone who wrote extremely well, who felt the horror of the drama deeply.

Martelly gave him a parting note just before he was called away, headed 'Last note on earth' in which he assured him that he died in faith and looked forward to meeting him in Heaven. He added at the final moment two words, blotched with tears, quickly scribbled beneath his signature. They were 'Excuse haste'.

In Andrews' family *The Spiritual Times* must have been read with much excitement, not only because it was his platform for many stories besides Martelly's, but more importantly because he owned it. Yet another wild extravagance like the Buckwell organ fitted in the chapel, it may have been for the glory of God, but it brought the family close to ruin. After only nine months it was forced to close through lack of support, 'much regretted by many readers'. That regret may still be shared, for in its four hundred pages there are wonderful examples of Andrews' style which so delighted his congregation; had it flourished, it might have contributed in many ways to our knowledge of Calvinistic oratory. 'Holy Spirit, Sweet Teacher, Charming Comforter,' he beseeched in *Family Prayer for Monday Morning*,[5] 'make our hearts thy long abode; let us know daily and hourly that thou art cleansing us from the love and power of sin; divorcing us from all self-righteousness, and hiding pride from our eyes . . .' He often wrote for the London Missionary Society of which a neighbour was Foreign Secretary:

Oh! let the Gospel go abroad; let angels pause as they fly along, to see our missionary ships sailing, and listen to the acclamations of earth, while heaven is absorbing all kingdoms into one: let us rejoyce that the world is beginning to awake: something else shall now be heard than the clarion of war, and the hoarse dull drum: men shall congregate for other purposes than murdering and disputing: the valleys shall hear thy name, O Jesus! and the mountains no longer be whitened with the bones of men; but covered with listening crowds: while the Holy Ghost hovers around and spreads millenial joy – stupendous rolls the anthem from a thousand hills, till, disturbed by the archangels' shout, it melts into the choirs of heaven! It is a pleasing thought, that we have lived to see that missionary age in which the Lord of Hosts is making his bow quite naked, and sending out unto all nations the lightening shafts of truth, not to destroy.[6]

The Andrews children also wrote for the magazine. Emily's eldest brother, Edward, contributed letters under the pseudonym of 'Verax'. In one of them, headed, *The Swiftness of Pigeons* about which he had read something in the newspapers, he drew a parallel to the speed of prayer, naturally enough echoing his father's manner. 'It is said that before an ordinary messenger could have reached a sea-port and fairly set sail, the letter is conveyed, and the answer received by means of two of these pigeons. Surely this should remind us of the sublime velocity with which prayer is acknowledged, that while the words are yet trembling on our lips, an answer of mercy is obtained.'[7]

The abrupt demise of *The Spiritual Times* in the early days of 1830 filled the children with consternation. Then they had a bright idea. They would edit a magazine by themselves. This they did for more than a year, writing almost every evening. It ended up in four volumes, each the size of a real book, each containing a hundred pages, proudly entitled *The Beresford Spy*, and now preserved as a family treasure. It was quite a feat, even then, when writing books in families was commonplace. One story was inspired by Emily who, at the time, was only six. The tale was about Emiliana, a poor orphan of great virtue who, after many trials, inherited her aunt and uncle's money. *The Spy* closed in 1831 after an elegant 'last bow' by the editor-in-chief, doubtless Edward, using the *nom de guerre* of 'The Visitor', better, he must have thought, than the earlier 'Verax'.

Emily's brothers, Edward and Frederic, the two eldest members of the family, both thoroughly enjoyed writing and later on both wrote accounts of their family and childhood. It is thanks to Edward that the present family can trace its links with many of its cousins – the Talfourds, Rutts, Gurneys, Hancocks – all families with distinguished members in the nineteenth century; and thanks to Frederic that something is known of Dr Andrews' house in Walworth where so many of them must have met.

The Chapel, of course, was the hub of the establishment, and its greatest pride, the magnificent organ. All Andrews' friends admired it and came to hear it whenever they could, whenever a virtuoso played there. In fact, it is not too much to say that the Beresford Chapel shared a part in the institution of the organ recital as a form of concert in its own right, which the Congregationalist movement sponsored. The resident organist was Frederic's mother; Frederic himself played it, too; and so did his eldest sister, Eliza. Music was part of all their lives. The house was full of musical instruments – pianos, horns and violins – all of which were played by Andrews. At musical evenings everyone took part. Eliza was the best at singing. Her rendering of 'Come where the aspens quiver' always held the room to silence, except on one dramatic occasion when it caused a guest, the Dean of Jersey, to break the spell with a gulp of genuine emotion.

Behind the organ was Andrews' study which was joined to the house by a private door – for the chapel and house were side by side. Here he would sit on winter evenings, reading, composing, playing, singing, and arguing with two dependent clergymen who had somehow managed to join the household. One was Danby, the other Popham, and both were old, rude and penniless. Frederic and his brother enjoyed tormenting them; but Andrews' heart was warm and large, and overflowed with love and patience for everyone.

In the house itself there was friendly chaos. Dozens of pictures covered the walls, family portraits and Claude-like landscapes; thousands of books were on all the shelves, in ancient as well as modern languages. They overflowed on to tables and chairs and made it hard, for guests especially, even to stand without disturbing them. In the summer, at least, things were easier. Behind the house was a splendid garden with extensive lawns and fine trees. Here the children learnt their lessons, were taught Latin and Greek by their mother, and raced about laughing and singing, distracting Dr Andrews who rushed from the vestry to tell them to be quiet but often, instead, joined their games. In the spring of 1831 the household numbered seventeen, three of whom were female servants, according to the fourth decennial census. One would have been a nurse, for little Clarence had just arrived, becoming the twelfth child of the family. The household was soon to be reduced. Within three months, three had died. 'My hand trembles while I write,' Dr Andrews noted in the Beresford Chapel Register as he entered little Clarence's death, 'yesterday morning (Sabbath) at six o'clock,' the 19th June, 1831. Little Lionel had died in May. Their mother had died on the 2nd of April. They were all buried in the same vault, next to her father at St Mary's Newington; the tiny coffins of the two infants resting on top of her own.

Dr Andrews' deep sorrow was tempered by real relief; not only because his wife's sufferings had come to an end at long last – she had died gradually from consumption – but also because his own burden had necessarily been erased. For his married life had not been a happy one. Amongst the thousands of Ruskin letters, which are now stored on the Isle of Wight, there is one from Ruskin's mother to his father which tells, almost in Andrews' words, how much his wife's behaviour had cost him.[8]

I was surprised on monday a little before eight at receiving a visit from Dr. Andrews [Mrs Ruskin wrote on the 10th March, 1831]. Fortunately I was up and just coming down to breakfast. He came he said to ask me what I thought of Mrs Andrews' state. She had another child about three weeks ago and has continued getting weaker ever since. She was so ill on Sunday that the Dr. did not preach. He gave me a long account of her complaints in the hope, I am certain, that I should say there was no chance of her living long. The Doctors say there is no hope of her. He also enlarged much on the torment she had been to him for these last ten years. It is altogether lamentable. I think the Dr. has wonderful talents – the way he ran on when giving John a little insight into the Hebrews on Monday. Much that I have seen of his readings in languages astonished me beyond all former measure, but he is certainly flighty, not to say more. In many respects his habits and manner of conducting his secular affairs, though with the best and kindest intentions, must to any woman with so numerous a family have caused much serious and distressing apprehension. This acting on a weak body and overwrought mind and, from what I can understand, the Doctors' unwise indulgence of every caprice, has occasioned such impatience and irritability as almost amounts to insanity and has made her the torment of herself and all about her. It is sad to think that the death of the Mother of thirteen★ living children should be looked forward to with pleasure even by her own husband and yet the history the Dr. gave of what he had endured from her caprice, jealousy, unreasonableness and violence, the way in which she has marred his respectability and fortune and prevented his filling that place in society his talents entitle him to, make one scarcely wonder at it. It would be better however if he said little about it except to real friends. It is imprudent, to say the least, saying so much to us [yet] knowing us so short a time – but I suppose he is glad to relieve his mind by any means.

Thus Mrs Andrews departed, not greatly regretted by her husband. At least her children mourned her differently. For them she had not been a difficult person; just a wonderful loving and adored mamma. Mrs Ruskin's reference to 'the Hebrews' and to Dr Andrews' 'wonderful talents' adverted to the fact that he was giving lessons to her son, John. Like many clergymen the learned doctor tutored pupils to increase his income, and two years earlier, in 1829, he had started teaching him Latin and Greek. In

★ Mrs Andrews had twelve living children – Mrs Ruskin is mistaken here.

that year John had been ten. He had liked Dr Andrews immediately. 'My dear papa,' he had written to his father, at that moment away on business,[9]

... the last three weeks and more may all be included in a most important aera of my life . . . namely the coming of the tutor for the first time. I believe few boys have a master who would say 'very well' when he had almost to tell him every word of a declension. What a nice man Doctor Andrews is, how I like him. What nice sermons he preaches. What a nice face he has, what a smiling noble frown he has. I do think, to use one of his own expressions, he looks best when he frowns, next when he laughs, and next when he neither frowns nor laughs. Every thing he does is nice, indeed it must be. What a nice way he has of teaching. But papa you will say that I am dwelling on the doctor too long so I shall take a jump.

He had written also to Mrs Monroe, the mother of Mrs Richard Gray, a friend and neighbour in Camberwell.[10]

Well, Papa, seeing how fond I was of the Doctor, and knowing him to be an excellent Latin scholar, got him for me as a tutor, and every lesson I get I like him better and better, for he makes me laugh 'almost, if not quite' – to use one of his own expressions – the whole time. He is so funny, comparing Neptune's lifting up the wrecked ships of Aeneas with his trident to my lifting up a potato with a fork, or taking a piece of bread out of a bowl of milk with a spoon! And he is always saying [things] of that kind, or relating some droll anecdote, or explaining the part of Virgil (the book which I am in) very nicely. I am always delighted when Mondays, Wednesdays and Fridays are come.

Both parents were pleased, too. In October 1829 Mrs Ruskin reported to her husband,[11]

John will send some exercises [in] my next letter. He laboured very hard at his Virgil and went over fifty lines to the Dr. yesterday (making only two mistakes), who was much pleased with him altogether. He comes tomorrow 20 minutes before 12. How I wished you had heard him on Sunday, I think he must be taking great pains with his sermons at present. I think I never heard one from him equal to that which he preached on Sunday morning. In the evening he said something on

cruelty to animals; he had been requested to preach by the society for
suppressing it. There were from 2 to 300 people could not get in.★ I
hope he will not be spoiled.

Dr Andrews did not get spoiled, as Mrs Ruskin feared he
might, but he did find by the following year that other commit-
ments to do with the chapel, not to speak of those to his wife who
at that time had not died, made his visits to the Ruskin household
more and more infrequent. Young John never forgot them.
They formed the basis of a friendship with Emily which later on
included her husband, and which lasted throughout his life.

After Mrs Andrews' death, family life at Beresford House, the
happy times that all the children remembered vividly for all their
lives, gradually came to an end. The first to leave the diminished
circle was Emily's eldest sister, Eliza. A year after her mother
died, Eliza married a neighbour, Charles Orme, the son of a
wealthy brewer. The eldest brother, Edward, then left to marry
a girl called Emily Bray. Then he and the next, Frederic, both set
sail for Australia in 1838. This was done from dire need. By then,
there was hardly enough money to go round to pay for the bare
necessities. Dr Andrews' financial affairs had reached a dangerous crisis. The extra problems of managing the family had taken
all his available time, the expenses of the Chapel had mounted
up, and a loyal attempt by the congregation to form a trust to buy
and manage it had failed to raise the necessary funds.

A member of his flock who knew him personally wrote about
him at this time.[12]

Those who knew Dr. Andrews intimately will not wonder at the
complications which eventuated in his leaving Beresford Chapel. Simple as a child in money matters, giving to a beggar a half-crown instead
of a penny, ready to write a cheque for any plausible applicant for relief,
and generally of unbounded hospitality, with a wife, equally learned,
who communed not with her household gods but with Homeric
Deities, and listened to the music of the spheres intermingled with the
prattle of her children; to such the finance of the household was not a
congenial study, and in the result the handsome Chapel and parsonage
had to be vacated for a less brilliant sphere.

★ There was seating for 1600 people in the Beresford Chapel.

This was the final, awful disaster. The Chapel was under a heavy mortgage. Quite suddenly the mortgagee, an untraced lady by the name of Kirwan, lost her patience and demanded payment. Mrs Kirwan seized her asset. There was nothing for it but to submit. A trust was formed, money collected, and a start made on a new building from which the Doctor's work could be carried on.

The Doctor, however, died of a heart attack only a few months afterwards. Since the Chapel had not been sold and was still capable of being used it was kindly lent for the conduct of his funeral. So on the 28th October, 1841 Edward Andrews, in his coffin, entered it through his private door and rested peacefully in it for the last time.

The Andrews family was now penniless. A collection even had to be made in the Chapel to meet the cost of the funeral. The children went to live with relations. All they had in the world to support them were their lost, happy, childhood memories. It was no mere figure of speech to say that they never forgot their parents. Years later they still talked of them, especially Frederic in distant Australia who composed recollections which pleased them all. He was not the stylist he wished to be, but nevertheless he wrote with sincerity. [13]

But when I forget my mother let my right hand forget its cunning. A more consummate domestic heroine never lived. Pious, amiable, indefatigable, always at home, always busy about our physical or mental welfare. She was a woman of very considerable talent, a hard student of ancient and modern languages, music and painting; all of which she laboriously taught her children; not meanwhile neglecting the careful consideration of humbler matters. If she had a fault it was in attending too rigidly to the systematic training of her family, to the exclusion of relaxation for herself, and sometimes of my poor father's company; so that I have heard him complain that while he gained a governess he lost a wife.

[About his father, Frederic wrote,] He was one of those comparatively few men who in their day and generation engross a large share of public attention in the great metropolis of England, one of those master spirits, who in the presence of every kind of excellence stand forth as stars of the first magnitude. His style of speaking and of preaching was such as I never heard from anyone else and cannot hope to do so; for it combined an easy conversational freedom with exalted sublimity and electrical fire.

On Sunday he assumed the highest walk of oratory. In the morning his elevated and classical discourses were more exclusively for his own people: in the evening when he had seldom less than fifteen or sixteen hundred hearers, they were of a more striking and diversified character, comprising every style and subject . . . and though he spoke for considerably upwards of a hour, I never knew anyone wish the sermon shorter . . . As he drew to a conclusion the dense mass around him was wrapt in a silence so breathless you could hear a pin fall to the ground; and when the last note of his sacred song was sung, they lingered long in place endeavouring to talk and think it all over again. He used to say that after an evening sermon he felt as if he had been up above the clouds in a balloon and wanted a parachute in which to descend gently and gradually.

Frederic's memoir was very long. Some of the others were rather shorter. Emily's sister, Eliza, the eldest girl of the family, the one who had married Charles Orme, kept a scrapbook throughout her life which is still a treasured possession of her descendants. In it, towards the end of the volume, she recorded her grief at her father's death. She only wrote one line, rather beautifully in black ink, using a fine quill pen.[14] 'October 19th 1871. This day, 30 years ago (Tuesday morning, Oct 19th 1841 at 3 o'clock) died our dear father. Still flows the bitter tear.' A decade later she did so again. 'We bitterly remember him in the day of battle. Wednesday evening Oct. 19 1881. Half past ten at night. His monument has been renovated this year.'* Thus his

---

* Dr Andrews' gravestone was removed and destroyed in 1971 by the Director of Civil Engineering and Public Services of the London Borough of Lambeth under the Borough's 'Lawn Conversion Plan'. The inscription on it read: 'In profound and grateful rememberance of the Revd Edward Andrews LL.D., Minister of Beresford Chapel, Walworth, this humble tribute is reared where his ashes rest. Born Jan 9th 1787 died Oct 19th 1841. He was an eloquent man and mighty in the scriptures, inflexibly attached to the doctrines of the Calvinistic school. Signally blessed by the Holy Ghost in his public ministration, gifted with persuasive oratory, with a high imagination and rare learning. Thus lofty in intellect, unassuming in manners, his character won the ardent love of all who knew him best, and moving among his fellow mortals but to comfort them, he saw in death not the end but the beginning.'

memory was kept alive and his tomb cleaned in Norwood cemetery as long as any of his children lived.

Eliza became the head of the Andrews family for the rest of her life; for the sons in Australia never returned, both becoming respectably prosperous and leaving many children and grand-children. As for the girls, Emily the 'Angel' and the next sister Georgiana, both went to live with Eliza, before they married into the same family, falling in love with two brothers. Emily, the elder married first according to the best Victorian tradition, Coventry Kersey Dighton Patmore.

CHAPTER THREE

Coventry's Father, Peter George

C OVENTRY PATMORE was born in Essex in the elegant surburban village of Woodford, eight miles north of London, on Wednesday 23 July, 1823. He was not baptised for nearly a year, until 11th June, 1824, as shown in the local Parish Register. His parents' abode was recorded as Woodford, without further identification; his father was named as Peter George and his occupation was given as 'Gent'; his mother, without her maiden name, was simply noted as Eliza. His baptismal name came from his godmother, the Hon. Mrs John Coventry, daughter-in-law of the 7th Earl of Coventry. She must have been a close friend for she gave him a fine silver cup; but she died only five years afterwards, and thus never fulfilled her role as spiritual guide and worldly benefactor.

His immediate family came from London, his grandfather being a jeweller and pawnbroker who, in 1783, had married Maria Clarissa Stevens. The occupation of her father, John, remains unknown; her mother, another Maria, was Dutch, a sister of the painter Gerhard Bockman, whose work survives at Hampton Court and the Gallery of Greenwich Hospital. In the last year of the 18th century the grandfather traded near St Paul's, at 33 Ludgate Hill, according to *Holden's Triennial Directory*. Selling watches without authority, he was forced to join the Clockmakers' Company, against his will as their history relates.[1] There he remained until 1820. Then he retired to live in Woodford which may account for Coventry's birth there. Nothing else is known of the family. Legend has it that early ancestors came from the village of Patmore Heath in Hertfordshire.

Coventry's father, Peter George, like Emily's father, Dr Andrews, was destined to leave a name behind him of much more interest now than anyone could have guessed at the time. Born in 1786, a year earlier than Dr Andrews, he went to a

The Patmore family

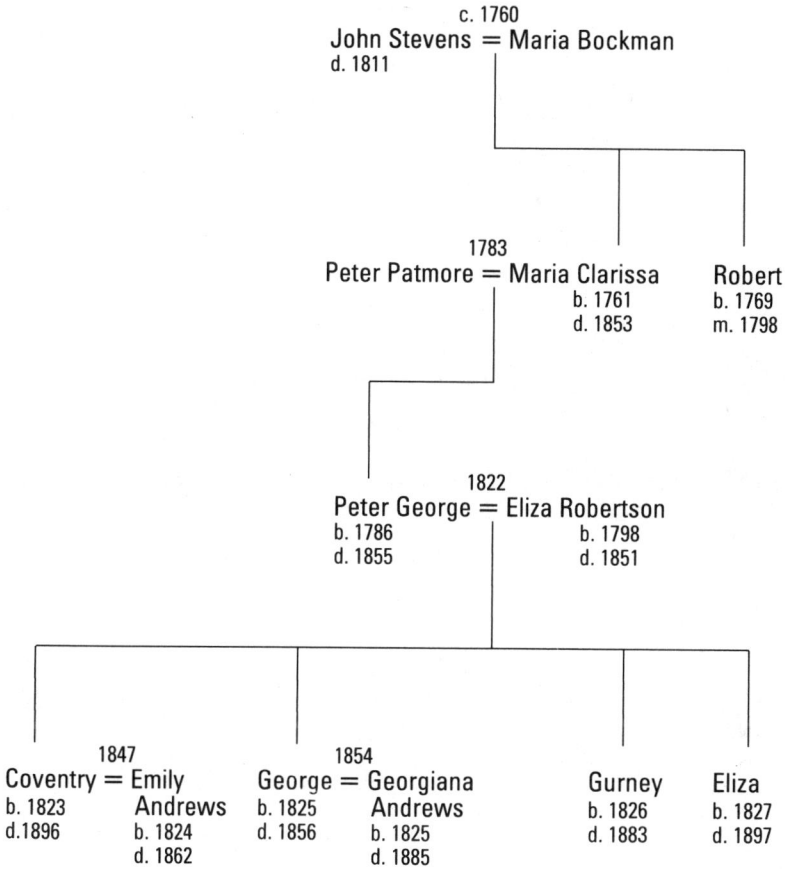

```
                              c. 1760
                    John Stevens = Maria Bockman
                    d. 1811
```

```
                        1783
              Peter Patmore = Maria Clarissa        Robert
                              b. 1761               b. 1769
                              d. 1853               m. 1798
```

```
                          1822
              Peter George = Eliza Robertson
              b. 1786       b. 1798
              d. 1855       d. 1851
```

1847		1854			
Coventry = Emily		George = Georgiana		Gurney	Eliza
b. 1823 Andrews		b. 1825 Andrews		b. 1826	b. 1827
d.1896 b. 1824		d. 1856 b. 1825		d. 1883	d. 1897
d. 1862		d. 1885			

boarding school at Woodford of which he left a nostalgic account, and then settled on Ludgate Hill to help his father run the business.[2] Trade, however, did not appeal to him. Like many another only child his parents spoilt him and gave him an allowance. He left home to live with friends and soon, in the manner of a 'Rake's Progress', found himself becoming a Dandy. The Dandy movement of that era, the early years of the 19th century, was one of those absurd crazes which sweep society from time to time and which ruin people who try to follow them without sufficient money to do so. Begun unwittingly by Beau Brummel, its followers aped his absurd manners, copied his fancy, extravagant clothes, exchanged insults with all who met them, and became, in the newspaper image of the day, a new breed of St James's reptile.

A self-portrait of Coventry's father, the only one that has managed to survive, done obviously at this period, shows him wearing the Dandy uniform, the high collar and frilled shirt which all the reptiles found obligatory. The movement quickly came to an end when the Beau went bankrupt and fled to Calais. Then Peter George grew up. He turned to his uncle, Robert Stevens, a man of ability, taste and knowledge, a Fellow of the Linnean Society of London, who had many friends in the learned world, and through him obtained a post as assistant manager at the Surrey Institution. This body, a kind of club, one of several founded then to enable men and women of culture to exchange ideas and hear lectures, had opened in 1808 in a fine building south of the Thames, just at the foot of Blackfriars Bridge, for the benefit of those who lived in the district. It did not survive for very long, closing in 1823, but while it flourished it provided a forum for all the leading lights of the day. Peter George got to know many of them: the great musician Dr Crotch; the famous inventor Goldsworthy Gurney; the celestial organist Samuel Wesley, a lifelong friend of Dr Andrews. Also he met William Hazlitt who gave his famous lectures on the English Poets, in the 1818 season. This was a meeting that was destined to have for Peter George and the unborn Coventry lasting, unhappy consequences.

Peter George had another interest besides the Institution. For some months he had been a journalist, and at the time of Hazlitt's lectures he was one of the London correspondents of *Blackwood's Edinburgh Magazine*. He wrote mainly about the play, his occasional *Notices of Acted Drama* being still of interest to theatre historians.[3] He enjoyed a free hand, however, and was able to write about anything he chose. He decided to report Hazlitt's lectures under, as usual, a *nom de plume* as all contributors did at that time, in this case 'A.Z.'.[4] His piece was liked by the *Blackwood's* management who, in an editorial poem addressed to him and other contributors, praised it as well as his drama notices.[5]

> Of pimpled Hazlitt's coxcomb lectures writing,
> Our friend with moderate pleasure we peruse.
> A.Z., when Kean's or Shakespeare's praise inditing,
> Seems to have caught the flame of either's muse.

Peter George should have been pleased, but in fact he was very annoyed, well knowing that William Hazlitt, who always resented personal attacks and whose face was as white as milk and quite unblemished by drink or disease, would be very upset by the adjective 'pimpled'. He wrote at once to William Blackwood.[6]

> By the bye, was it not a gratuitous piece of *imprudence* (to say the least of it) to admit that line in the last No. about 'pimpled Hazlitt'? In consequence of being one of the Managers of a Literary Institution I have been led to form a slight personal acquaintance with Mr. Hazlitt, & I have reason to know that such notices as that to which I allude are exceedingly obnoxious to him & I suppose your editor is not ignorant how tremendous his power is when he sets about to resent what he feels or fancies to be an injury.

Blackwood answered three days later.[7] 'We received your articles just in time. They are very interesting. Your communications are much liked here. As to the line on W. Hazlitt I believe it was put in without thought and I am sure if the Editor had considered it, he would have altered it.' Likely enough this was the truth and Peter George in his next article did his best to make amends.[8] 'By the bye, what can our Editor's facetious friend mean by "pimpled Hazlitt"? If he knows that gentleman's person, he cannot intend the epithet to apply to *that*; and how "pimpled" may be interpreted with reference to *mind*, we are not able to divine. A.Z.'

Hazlitt, however, hypersensitive almost to the point of monomania, could not be placated. He felt he had been unjustly insulted and feared the effect on his reputation – rightly so, since the adjective stuck and ever since has been linked with his name. Thus Peter George's article which, of course, remained anonymous, through no fault of his own was instrumental in giving Hazlitt the famous obnoxious epithet. A.Z. kept his secret. It was, however, for Peter George a source of real regret for the rest of his life.

A little later on in the year he was able to some extent to make amends. Hazlitt belonged to the literary circle which *Blackwood's* had christened the Cockney School, the leader of which was Leigh Hunt (in contra-distinction to the Lake School, the circle of Wordsworth, Coleridge and Southey). Leigh Hunt was also a poet, and had recently published *The Story of Rimini*, an historical tale of adultery and incest which had taken place in the 13th century. *Blackwood's* had savagely torn it to pieces. Hazlitt had liked it and written a review, calling it 'fresh, lively and artless', in a rival magazine, *The Edinburgh*. Therefore *Blackwood's* turned on Hazlitt.

In a sneering article the following August the editor accused him of immorality and wanton, gross, indecent quackery.[9] This was positively quite mild compared to the attacks on Leigh Hunt, but, as Peter George had warned, Hazlitt could not be insulted lightly. He immediately sued for slander. In public Blackwood laughed this off, but in private he wrote to Peter George to ask him to try to settle it discreetly.[10] 'I need not say how much I shall feel indebted to you if you are successful in your mediation. I am sure that, if you are, you will be doing both Mr. Hazlitt and me a real service, but, if not, it will not I know be your fault, and it cannot be helped – we are prepared well, and matters must just take their course.'

Peter George accomplished his mission, obtaining for Hazlitt damages and costs. Both parties thanked Peter George warmly. Hazlitt became an accepted friend; Blackwood, however, became an enemy of Peter George. After a pause Blackwood attacked again, and became involved in a feud with another member of the Cockney School which even Peter George was unable to stop.

In the summer of 1820, a member of the group, John Scott, who felt keenly that *Blackwood's* methods were debasing the standard of English literature, decided to take up the Cockney cause and attack the *Blackwood's* editors himself. Peter George, who knew him well, writing with more vision than he realised, warned him that such a move was dangerous. He wrote to Scott, speaking of the editors.[11]

... There's no denying that they are very powerful fellows. To be sure it is not exactly the kind of power one would like to possess but it is very *effective* nevertheless. Half of it (& that half one *would* like to possess) is the power of real talent – but the other half is the power of men reckless of cause & consequences. It is the power that a man who chooses to set his life 'at a pin's fee' possesses, & may safely exercise over the lives of others.

John Scott ignored this warning. He ran the new *London Magazine* to which Peter George contributed as well as other more distinguished writers, notably Hazlitt and Charles Lamb. In a series of long and bitter articles he attacked *Blackwood's* from every standpoint, especially the use of anonymity in making cowardly attacks on others just to increase their circulation.[12]

If the writers in *Blackwood's Magazine* possess talents for satire and ridicule, let them exert these – but let them be fairly exerted. What we complain of is, that, by a series of tricks and impositions, unknown to criticism and literary discussion before their career, they have outraged private character, prostituted principle, insulted decency, perverted truth, and exhibited a spectacle of venal and spiteful buffoonery under the name of literature, to the corruption of taste, and the gratification of the worst feelings.

Scott concluded by identifying 'Z', also known as 'Olinthus Petre'. To flush him out he called him a coward. No man at that time could accept an insult of that nature unless he wished to be shunned for the rest of his life.

The editor named was John Gibson Lockhart, the son-in-law of Sir Walter Scott and destined to write his superb biography, who, because of the deadly sting with which he poisoned many of his articles, was known in the literary world as 'The Scorpion'. He took the coach to London at once to obtain an apology from John Scott or else to be given 'satisfaction', in other words to fight a duel with pistols. Due to a muddle nothing was settled, so John Lockhart, whose wife was pregnant and expected confinement at any moment, returned to Edinburgh the next day. He left a friend called Jonathan Christie to contact Scott to explain his departure. Scott thought that Lockhart had retreated, and openly said he had scuttled away instead of remaining in London to see him. Christie defended Lockhart and denied it. He accused Scott of lying and shuffling. Scott retorted by issuing a challenge – addressed to Christie, not to Lockhart. Against his will, Christie felt in honour bound to accept it. So the two prepared to fight. Neither had ever done so before or knew anything about the rules and practice of duelling.

Peter George at this moment was having an amusing time at Bath. 'My Dear Scott', he wrote to his friend on 26th December, 1820, in a letter partly addressed to the wife to whom he had a cheerful attachment not, it was thought, entirely disinterested,[13]

I am living here in the strangest & most superfluous way that you can imagine – doing everything in the most coxcomical of styles – dressing like a coxcomb – talking like a coxcomb – thinking like a coxcomb – writing like a coxcomb – in short I'm afraid I really *am* a coxcomb. Don't you think I am? And yet I can't help persuading myself that if I was anything *but* one I should not now be in a situation to ask *you* the question & above all I should not feel myself entitled, & should therefore not dare – as I do now – to subscribe myself

Always sincerely yours

P. G. PATMORE

The letter came to Scott's hand right in the middle of his row with Christie. He was just about to issue his challenge. For this purpose he needed a Second. Very unwisely he turned to Peter George, who had many qualities – taste, charm, ease of manner – but not those required of a Second. These were stated quite succinctly by a military man named Abraham Bosquett who had fought in four duels himself and been a Second in twenty-five.[14]

Then, let your Second be, if such can be had, a man of honor, a man of sense, cool, but determined that you shall acquit yourself honorably. But if he is beside a man of experience, of conciliating and pursuasive address, so much the better. In such a man's hands fatal consequences seldom ensue: and I am pursuaded, from my own experience, that in many duels where the issue has proved disastrous, 'tis one or other of the Seconds, and often both that ought to be hanged, and not the surviving Principal.

In practical terms the Second's task was simple and quite straightforward. Once negotiations had failed, and the time, place and weapons had been chosen, he had only to stand beside his Principal not (of course, in the line of fire) and ensure by the strictest possible observance that nothing happened beyond the rules. Briefly put, these were as follows: first, to fire when the signal was given – not, obviously, to do so earlier; second, to fire again if necessary, if both parties had missed their aim and when both Seconds had obtained agreement. Here there was one important exception. If either party had 'fired away' or, as the jargon had it '*deloped*', that is to say had missed on purpose, then the contest came to an end. On this the manuals were quite specific:[15]

Upon a *delope* the affair immediately terminates, and the Second should never permit another discharge. When a man fires in the air, it is considered an acknowledgement that he has been in fault; and although he may still refuse to make an apology, the opposite party has no right to demand another fire: he has 'given satisfaction'.

The flowery meadows by Chalk Farm, with Primrose Hill rising behind them, where Scott and Christie decided to meet, were a favourite place for settling disputes in the early years of the 19th century. A mile and a half from Tottenham Court and easy to reach, being close to the road, they were safely out of the way of the law, but near enough to civilization in the case of any emergency. A bright moon lit the scene as Scott and Christie arrived on the ground, although a slight fog or mist made the air seem hazy. At the first fire, no one fell. The pistols therefore were re-loaded and the Principals stood to fire once more. At this point, according to the evidence, Christie's Second shouted to Christie that he must, this time, take his aim. Scott heard him and lowered his arm, knowing the rule about deloping and thinking the contest must be over. He turned to confer with Peter George. The latter, out of excitement or ignorance, told Scott not to speak and that he had no option but to shoot, 'you have nothing for it but the firing.'

Scott did so but missed again. Christie, furious, returned the fire. Scott fell, shot in the stomach. He was carried to the inn at Chalk Farm. The bullet was removed but the wound festered. He was never able to leave his bed and died at the Farm, his wife beside him, less than a fortnight afterwards. Peter George was aghast. He wrote to his mother.[16]

If he dies I lose the dearest friend I ever had, among men. My sorrow and affliction are more than it is possible to express. All things that ever happened to me before are nothing, compared with this last fatal misfortune. I am stricken to the ground. For the first time in my life I confess that Fate or Fortune, or whatever it may be, has been too strong for me. It is as much – it is almost more than I can do, to struggle against it. But I must and will. You and Eliza* must come up to me.

When Scott expired Peter George as well as Christie and the latter's Second fled to France to avoid arrest. They were all charged, according to the law, on the basis of *prima facie* evidence, with the crime of 'wilful murder'.

Peter George's partiality towards Scott's wife – a Second admiring a Principal's spouse was a well known cause of mischief – was not forgotten by observant enemies. Although he was cleared of the charge of murder at the subsequent trial at the Old Bailey, he was not forgiven for staying in France when the others accused returned to attend it. This was a final, grave mistake. It appeared to show an admission of guilt.

The literary world was extremely hostile. 'What a terrible

---

* His future wife.

affair this duel is!' wrote Mary Russell Mitford, the immortal authoress of *Our Village*.[17]

What a pity that poor John Scott did not at once fight Mr. Lockhart with Horace Smith for his second; or, which would have been better still, say firmly that he would not fight at all in a literary quarrel. He is now the victim of his own contemptible second; a man who is a pawnbroker on Ludgate Hill and a dandy in St. James's Street; and who egged on his unhappy friend to gratify his own trumpery desire of notoriety. I hope he will be severely dealt with.

In private, this was the general verdict. In public the matter was soon forgotten. A fund was opened for Scott's widow who was left penniless with two children. *Blackwood's* helped to collect the money, but never acknowledged any regret or gave Scott even a short obituary.

There the matter might have closed and the bitter war against the Cockneys allowed to come to a halt. Possibly this might have come to pass if *Blackwood's* had not had a stroke of luck two years later. This gave them such a marvellous chance to blow the Cockney School to bits that they felt they really could not resist it. It was the publication by Hazlitt of a book called *Liber Amoris*. 'The Book of Love' or *The New Pygmalion*, which appeared in May, 1823, pretended to be an anonymous account of a fatal passion for a simple girl, told by the man to whom it had occurred, who had since died of a broken heart. Composed in the manner of the 18th century as a series of letters and conversations, in fact the story was Hazlitt's own. He had fallen in love with his landlord's daughter who was twenty-four years younger than himself and, of course, had been rejected. This explains the alternative title: Pygmalion was the sculptor who fell in love with a statue. Only a few days elapsed before his enemies found him out and his authorship was known.

The book, too, was extremely silly, although it included some fine passages. These were contained in the lover's letters, some of which were addressed to the girl, and some to a friend called 'C.P.'. As soon as Hazlitt's name was disclosed, it was extremely easy to work out who these two were. The girl proved to be

Sarah Walker, the younger daughter of the house he lodged in; 'C.P.', 'My Dear Friend', turned out to be Peter George.

The book's fault was its sexuality. In contemporary terms it was highly indecent, the letters showing Hazlitt's behaviour was devious, prurient and unashamed. Once it was known to be a true story, revealing Hazlitt's inner thoughts – how he had loved Sarah and hated her, how he had actually got a divorce to try to force her hand in marriage, and how, on failure, he had asked a friend, usually thought to be Peter George, to try to take her virginity for him – the popular condemnation was unanimous.

Peter George, to give him his due, appears to have done his best to make Hazlitt calmer. The latter had written to Peter George,[18]

You say it is my own 'outrageous conduct' that has estranged her; nay, I have been *too gentle* with her. I ask you first in candour whether the ambiguity of her behaviour with respect to me, sitting and fondling a man (circumstanced as I was) sometimes for half a day together, and then declaring she had no love for him beyond common regard, and professing never to marry, was not enough to excite my suspicions . . . My unpardonable offence has been that I took her at her word, and was willing to believe her the precise little puritanical person she set up for. After exciting her wayward desires by the fondest embraces and the purest kisses . . . I did not proceed to gratify them, or to follow up my advantage . . . Yet anyone but a credulous fool like me would have made the experiment . . .

Blackwood's pounced with the utmost delight, quite unable to contain itself.[19]

Good public, since we first took pen in hand, nothing so disgusting as this has ever fallen in our way. We have gone through with it, because we conceived that not to do so would be a most serious breach of public duty in a journal which may trace five-sixths of all vulgar abuse that has been heaped upon its character and conduct to this one single fact, that IT HAS EXPOSED AND RUINED THE COCKNEY SCHOOL.

We leave 'H——' in the hands . . . of the British public; and we call down upon his head, and upon the heads of those accomplished reformers in ethics, religion, and politics, who are now enjoying his *chef-d'oeuvre*, the scorn and loathing of every thing that bears the name of MAN. Woman! – But it would be an insult to go further.

All that remained for Peter George, after similar outbursts appeared in all the major journals, using terms like 'nauseous', 'revolting', and 'disgusting', was to find his name included, too. In *John Bull* he unhappily did so.[20]

We honestly confess, that if MR. HAZLITT's proceedings had ended with his acquaintance with little SALLY we should never have disturbed him in his exalted pursuit, but have considered the young lady as one of the pleasantest *little Sallies* we had ever fallen in with when thinking about him; but the *fellow brags* – writes to MR. PATMORE , a pawn-broker's son, who, alas! was second to the MR. SCOTT, who was shot in a duel, and brags of his intimacy, etc, with this unoffending girl. We say, why should this young woman be calumniated? – why should the disappointed dotard – the impotent sensualist – gratify the only passion he has it in his power to enjoy, SPITE, at the expense of this young woman?

Thus Hazlitt's *Liber Amoris* really damaged Peter George, and what was worse, his children, too. Long after Hazlitt's death, whenever his books were reprinted, whenever contemporary memoirs were published, whenever biographers wrote his life, the sordid story was told again, each time more unpleasantly. For other papers began to appear – the journal of Sarah, Hazlitt's wife, and complete texts of Hazlitt's letters, many of which had never been published, which hinted at Peter George's involve-ment in a manner more salacious than ever. Added to which, Victorian standards, deploring any sexual levity and applauding only marital love, caused the book to be seen as pornography, not as a nympholeptic fit – the frenzy of one who has seen an unattainable nymph – a mere aberration of the spirit of one to whom honour was due as a great master of the English language.

For Peter George's son, Coventry, *Liber Amoris* proved an embarrassment that only grew as time went on. 'Unwholesome rubbish', he used to declare it, doing his best to repair the damage and forgive his father for a youthful folly. He tried in vain; for in 1902, almost a decade after his death, Augustine Birrell, writing of Hazlitt, called the episode up again. 'Vile kitchen stuff,' he wrote, 'only fit to be thrown on the midden.' Of Peter George he was equally dismissive. 'The un-desirable Patmore' he called him. Nothing Coventry ever wrote was able to excuse his father's conduct or repair the damage it did to himself and the family's reputation.

After these two disasters, Scott's death and *Liber Amoris*, Peter George settled down to lead the life of a busy journalist, editing books and periodicals including the *New Monthly*, of which he was sub-editor for twelve years. By nature warm, gregarious and talkative, he continued to live in the literary world of Hazlitt, Charles Lamb and the Hunts, as well as others unremembered, whose names then were household words. He appears in many memoirs of the time, but usually only hidden in a footnote. In the later years he wrote about his contemporaries, but very few of them bothered to write about him. He does, however, emerge occasionally. The artist Northcote praised his judgement; the publisher Ollier recalled his honesty as well as his intellectual endowments; Charles Lamb, in an introductory letter, said he was a 'hearty, friendly fellow'. Carew, grandson of William Hazlitt, also added a line to the picture, describing Peter George at Hendon, then a hilly, breezy paradise, where the latter had rented a comfortable house with a large meadow and a kitchen garden. Peter George at that time had plenty of work and a wife with money. Here he wrote his best book, his *Imitations of Celebrated Authors*, as well as others now forgotten. He enjoyed playing the part of the squire, wandering round his miniature estate, selling the hay and counting the apples. Carew liked him and thought him 'original'. Looking back at the end of his life, Peter George must have considered these as his happiest days.

In August, 1822, eighteen months after the duel, he had married a girl he knew well, Eliza Robertson, his mother's companion. Described as 'a lady of some beauty' she came from Scotland with a modest fortune, the daughter of a Henry Robertson of Perth, about whom nothing is known.[21] Here at Hendon, and further east along the road in Woodford Green, where Peter George's parents lived as well as his uncle Robert Stevens, Eliza brought up her four children: Coventry, George, Gurney and Eliza.

Concerning the mother, little has survived. There are no letters, no portraits, and only a conversational tribute in one of

Peter George's books, *The Mirror of the Months*, published four years after their marriage, a series of essays in calendar form. Her birthday fell in the month of February, and in his piece about that time he compared her virtues to those of others, also born in the shortest month, naturally enough to her advantage. She was wise, observant and 'softly sweet', more so than Bacon, Galileo and Handel, his choice of eminent Februarians. In fact she was said to be stern and cold, a true daughter of the vilest month, with a strictly puritan love of God and an equally rigid approach to her children. She was fond of Peter George however, and seems to have made him a capable wife. Many a time in the years ahead when lawsuits pressed and markets crashed he must have blessed the day when first he met her.

As time passed, the clouds gathered. Much of the family money was spent, and the four children had to be educated. Peter George was working for Colburn, the owner of various magazines, one of which was the *Court Journal*. When acting as editor of this, Peter George carelessly libelled the Duchess of Richmond. He said she had run away with an officer, a tale that proved to be quite untrue. The full weight of ducal wrath fell upon Peter George's head, and although in law he was not to blame, nevertheless he had to suffer as though he had been. He forfeited a large sum of money and lost his job on the *Journal* as well. Like many another contemporary innocent, he tried to recoup by investing in railway shares but the market in them crashed in 1845 and he lost everything. He fled to France to avoid his creditors, leaving Coventry with almost nothing. Coventry was twenty-two and two years later he met his Emily. Both had seen their families collapse from comparative wealth to absolute poverty. This must have formed, from the very start, an immediate bond between them.

Peter George returned to England, after a penniless spell in Calais under the names of Pitt and Preston, to cause his son a last embarrassment. He had always been of a sociable nature, and over the years had known people in all walks of artistic life, so he decided to publish his personal memoirs. These appeared in 1854 under the title of *My Friends and Acquaintance*. At once they provoked widespread criticism. Written in polished journalese and filled with sometimes racy gossip and many extracts from private letters, they ignored the prevailing literary demand for elegant prose and harmless anecdote, supplying instead cheerful accounts of how his friends had actually lived. Amongst these were Charles Lamb, the Countess of Blessington, Thomas Campbell, Laman Blanchard and, of course, William Hazlitt. To include the last was bad enough. Far worse, there was a seventeen-page chapter full of sympathy and understanding, without a word of remorse or apology, about *Liber Amoris*.

The editor of the *Athenaeum* wrote, 'We shall make a long skip over Mr. Patmore's revelations and recollections of Hazlitt – not merely because we have met many of them before, but because we must think that the disregard here shown to survivors is best and most gravely animadverted on by silence – not the silence of "consent".'[22] After hearing from dozens of subscribers who had read the book and then written to him the editor added, three weeks later, 'The judgement of *The Athenaeum* on Mr. Patmore's book as a miscellany carelessly made up, containing praise without sufficient ground, impeachment without warrant, and anecdotes of doubtful character, seems to be shared by persons in all circles of London Society.'[23] The timing of this could not have been worse. Coventry, too, was publishing a book, the first volume of his *Angel in the House*, his poem on pure and legitimate love. To avoid disgrace by association, with poor reviews and sales in consequence, he took the only available course, removed his name from the title page, and issued the work anonymously.

It has to be said that Peter George sought and kept Hazlitt's friendship to the last, in spite of the shadow of *Liber Amoris* and his extremely difficult character. Hazlitt's grandson wrote about him,[24]

... if I were to name the person whose intimacy, in my own opinion, was of the greatest service to him [Hazlitt] from 1820–1830, I should name Mr. Patmore. There was a striking intellectual inequality between the two, and it was this very inequality which cemented the union – an union which, after all, it is not so difficult to understand. Mr. Hazlitt tolerated Mr. Patmore till he liked him.

Hazlitt died in 1830. Nobody bothered about his work, and his life appeared to have been a failure. He had known many people in his time but only two came to his funeral, Charles Lamb and Peter George. For this, literary history honours them. Also, for months after his death, at great inconvenience to himself, Peter George helped to settle his affairs.

A postscript remains on Hazlitt's death, this time involving the Andrews family. Emily's elder brother, Frederic Andrews, had always longed to become an author and had always considered William Hazlitt to be the finest writer of his time. He worshipped the essayist's every word, and when he learnt of Hazlitt's death he went immediately to his hero's house and begged the housekeeper to let him in to pay his last respects to the corpse. Hazlitt lay in a small coffin. Frederic, deeply moved by the sight, impulsively seized his right hand and, for a moment, pressed it reverently. 'The hand,' as he wrote, 'that had launched so many thunders of invective and entwined so many garlands of beautiful passionate eulogy.' Then he took as a souvenir Hazlitt's little glass inkwell and a bundle of sheets of corrected manuscript. Back at the Andrews' home in Walworth, Emily must have seen these treasures. Later on, when she was engaged, she must have talked about them to Coventry. Thus Hazlitt's reputatation made its mark on both their families.

Years afterwards Frederic wrote about it. By then he was far away in Australia, all his possessions safely with him. His story is prosy and sentimental, on a large sheet of blue paper, watermarked 1853, part of a long account of his childhood which he made towards the end of his life. He composed in ink with a fine pen dipped, no doubt, in Hazlitt's inkwell. Even then it was still undamaged. All these years he had kept it carefully. Wanting his children to know what it was so that they, too, could treasure it as he had, he also explained the reason for its excellent condition. He had kept it clean and quite unscratched, having, he said with pride, 'for full security, had it cased in tin'.

Peter George's own death took place in 1855, a year after *My Friends and Acquaintance* had so upset his family. In May the *North British Review* had given him yet another rebuke. In a long study of a comparable work, *The Literary Life of the Countess of Blessington*, the reviewer had said, 'It is a better book than Mr.

Patmore's . . . because its morality is more endurable, and its impertinence less; but it resembles in many respects that objectionable work . . .' His wife had expired three years previously. Once very cheerful and talkative, in old age he became silent. He died while staying with Coventry and Emily at their house in Highgate, 8, The Grove, thus ending a busy but often misdirected life. Even his going was inconvenient. He passed away on Christmas Day at twenty minutes past one in the afternoon, so spoiling all the planned festivities. His three grandchildren had to be quiet, and sighs rustled in the little house which should have rung with Coventry's and Emily's laughter.

CHAPTER FOUR

Coventry Meets and Weds his Angel

COVENTRY'S early childhood in the middle years of the 1820s, before he was old enough for school, was spent at Epping with his grandmother, widow of the pawnbroker Peter Patmore, and also with her brother, Robert Stevens. Coventry was happy and loved them both. His grandmother spoilt him without shame, an extra joy since he feared his mother who was cold, stern and authoritarian. Artistic, warm and intelligent, Grandmother Patmore taught him how to read and write and also, as the fashion was for little boys as well as girls, the manual skills of knitting and sewing. As he worked she told him tales of thrilling battles long ago or frightening stories of the Gordon Riots of which she had been an eye-witness. His first words, under her tuition, were 'Coventry is a clever fellow'.

His great-uncle also spoilt him and opened his mind to the wider world, describing countries far away and taking him off for picnics in the forest, still the haunt of highwaymen and gypsies, giving him enchanting lessons in botany. Robert Stevens has left his mark as Secretary of the London Institution, and as a Fellow of the Linnean Society of London. According to tradition he travelled widely, collected flowers, and drew and painted them. None of his works seems to have survived. His love of nature did so, however, in being handed down to Coventry and years afterwards revived and given a measure of immortality in some of the latter's finest poetic passages.

Coventry's subsequent education was undertaken by Peter George. Most of the days he simply read, under his father's general direction. He studied science as well as literature, and being rather bookish by nature and able to work by himself for hours, he was well grounded in many subjects by the time he reached his fifteenth birthday. He only went to school once, in Paris at the age of sixteen. He was meant, of course, to learn the language but he spent most of his time with the English, friends of his father, like Mrs Gore, the prolific authoress who kept a salon. He fell in love with her daughter Cecilia, to learn from her, for the first time, the pain of an unrequited attachment. Naturally enough he missed his family who did their best to keep him in touch. His father's letters were as long as novels and full of tedious, sensible advice. His grandmother's notes were more to the point. She missed him as much as he missed her.[1]

Pentonville, 10th Oct., 1839.

MY DEAREST DEAR COVENTRY

I think of you every Day, and *every* hour but particularly every Sunday; a beautiful day in France; the people all look so happy – and you are more so on that day – because you have your liberty, *think* if I could be with you one Sunday and walk in the Forest, and see *Paris*. I thank you, my dearest for the beautiful little views. I look at *them* and read your *letter every* day. I will take your advice and make myself as happy as I can without you, and you have a *Friend*; how delightful to meet with such a treasure at such a distance from home, you must tell him, I am sure I should like him, because he is *your Friend*. I am quite well but it is very cold *here* – so exposed to the north winds.

I am as ever your own Dear, Dear Granny,

C. M. PATMORE

Coventry returned to England in 1840. He had learnt some French, a little German, and how to practice the art of fencing. He had also learnt to dislike the Parisians, perhaps because he had been so homesick, a bias which he felt for the rest of his life. He was now aged seventeen and had to think about what to do, what career to adopt to make a living. He thought of going up to Cambridge with a view to taking Holy Orders, but even then, before the crash, found that his father could not afford it. He was clever and gifted in several directions. He liked mathematics, was good at chemistry, understood architecture, appreciated art, and enjoyed literary composition. For a time he worked at each in turn, solving mathematical problems, using a basement for chemical experiments, learning design and structure in buildings, absorbing the principles of painting and drawing, studying the rules of drama and poetry.

He was best, he found, at painting and writing. A sketch he

submitted to the Society of Arts, a copy of one of Landseer's animals, gained a prize, a Silver Palette, in one of its annual competitions. Some of his verses were read aloud to an evening gathering at his home, and two were voted by Laman Blanchard, a well-respected literary critic who was also a friend of the Andrews family, to be extremely beautiful and finished. They were called 'The River' and 'The Woodman's Daughter.'

In the end, literature claimed him. Reading Tennyson's latest poems, which were published in 1842 and included the epic *Morte d'Arthur*, made him realise his true vocation and see clearly the path ahead. Inspired by the magic and music of words, with all the passion and sentiments of youth, he rejected the hope of material gain which he might have had from regular employment and determined to become a poet.

Peter George was delighted when Coventry told him of this decision. As soon as Coventry had written more, adding two longer narrative pieces, one modelled on Boccacio's *Falcon*, the other a tale of rejected love in the manner of Tennyson's *Locksley Hall*, Peter George sent them to Moxon the publisher, and later posted copies of the finished book to all his friends.

To his great joy, everyone liked them. 'They are indeed beautiful, and as fresh and original as beautiful ...' wrote the Countess of Blessington, the fashionable novelist, adding that she looked forward to meeting the author.[2] 'The subject of The Woodman's Daughter is painful, but it is very cleverly and delicately treated,' commented Horatio Smith, the celebrated essayist.[3] 'Did you read The River by Patmore?' Anne Procter, the literary hostess, asked Richard Monckton Milnes. 'It is the most perfect of any of his poems.'[4] Milnes wrote to Anthony Panizzi, the Keeper of Printed Books in the British Museum, 'I maintain they are of the highest genius.'[5] Giving praise where praise was due, many of Peter George's friends awarded credit to him, also. 'I congratulate you sincerely on a son of such indisputable genius, and such brilliant promise,' Bulwer Lytton told him, enclosing at the same time a long letter of constructive criticism addressed directly to Coventry.[6]

Peter George's literary enemies read his offspring's poems, too, with much glee and satisfaction. Never since *Liber Amoris*, which had been in print for a quarter of a century, had they hit upon such a glorious chance to renew their attack on Peter George and the whole poetic movement he stood for. In September, 1844, *Blackwood's* devoted eleven pages to tearing every poem to pieces. Coventry was damned for the 'weakest inanity', 'nauseous pulings', 'feculant folly', and 'vapid silliness'; as a perfect example of the Cockney School which the editor thought he had managed to strangle years before when reviewing Hazlitt. A real literary battle began, with enemies following *Blackwood's* footsteps, and friends rushing to Coventry's defence. *Punch* fought nobly for Coventry. It noted ironically,[7]

The *Spectator* of Sunday last put its icy paw upon the poets who publish with Mr. Moxon. Among these genii, be it remembered, is Alfred Tennyson, the writer of *Locksley Hall* ... To these – he is glorious company; and, more, is worthy of it – the *Spectator* adds, Mr. Coventry Patmore, a very young writer, who has just given to the world a small volume of poems – full of various beauty – a volume we heartily recommend to all men.

In the *English Review* a year later he was given a notice beside the stars – Elizabeth Barrett and Robert Browning.[8] They had both read his poems, and liked them.[9] Elizabeth Barrett had granted them 'power', Robert Browning had thought them a 'great and – for a man of twenty – wonderful success'.[10] By then Coventry had met him at one of Anne Procter's parties. In such company he felt accepted, the battle won and his choice vindicated.

Except for a journey to Edinburgh to visit his aunts, his mother's sisters, he stayed at home and worked seriously, looking ahead, not unreasonably, for real glory in the course of time. Then, suddenly, a note from France informed him of Peter George's bankruptcy. Coventry had no money and a small cheque, enclosed with the letter, represented a last allowance. After that, it was destitution, unless he could earn a living as a hack or somehow, somewhere, manage to find a patron. All the friends rallied round him. Thackeray introduced him to *Fraser's* magazine; *Punch* published some topical verses; other journals accepted articles which gave him just enough to live on. Still, the future looked unpromising. Anne Procter reported to Milnes in November, 1844, 'I saw Coventry Patmore yesterday looking very well and very anxious to begin and work – but how? and where?'[11]

Monckton Milnes, as a Member of Parliament, knew something that Anne Procter did not – that the British Museum was short of money and that the government planned to give it some more. The extra funds were for extra staff. Those brought in would work in the library, especially in modernising the catalogue about which there had been complaints from every reader who had ever used it. One, for example, had written in *The Times*,[12]

> In the reading room of the British Museum are 25 folio volumes of written catalogue, descriptive of nearly 10,000 manuscripts, one half of which was deposited there full 100 years since, and the remainder previous to the year 1835. Perhaps some of your many correspondents will have the goodness to inform me and my brother readers, through the medium of your valuable paper, why they have been allowed to remain until this day unindexed? Some thousands are voted annually for the use of the institution, of which I presume, the library department receives its due share; yet the numerous readers are daily put to the inconvenience of wading through the whole of the above-mentioned 25 volumes before they can attain to that information which a faithful index would convey at a single glance.

As well as being a Member of Parliament, Milnes moved in the world of books. He liked helping young writers, in Coventry's case the more especially for having been a rare supporter of Peter George and *Liber Amoris*, a work he had actually called 'delightful'.[13] He knew how to go about it and wrote to the Archbishop of Canterbury, a Trustee of the British Museum, to ask if a place could be found for Coventry. Then he wrote to Anthony Panizzi to ask him to grant the poet an interview. The result was recorded in the Trustees' Minutes for 28th November, 1846. 'The Secretary reported that the Principal Trustees had nominated Mr. Zedner, and Mr. Coventry Patmore to be two of the additional Supernumerary Assistants in the Department of Printed Books.'[14] Their salary was to be £128 per annum. They were both to work on the catalogue. As well as bringing it up to date they had to get it ready for printing, a task already behind schedule and not to be finished for half a century. When they began it had only reached the letter 'C'. Oddly enough, the word in hand was none other than 'Coventry'.

In the meantime, while waiting, Coventry had shyly courted Emily. They had met earlier through Laman Blanchard whose admiration for Coventry's poems had prompted Peter George to publish them. Since then, they had kept in touch. After Dr Andrews' death, on which Blanchard had written an ode, still treasured in the family scrapbook, Emily had gone to live in Hampstead. There, in a house in Avenue Road, a much loved young aunt to a growing family of boys and girls, she had stayed with her eldest sister, Eliza, wife of the prosperous brewer and distiller, Charles Orme. Eliza Orme's education as well as her youthful friendship with families like the Ruskins had given her a taste for artistic people. Having the means through her marriage, she was able, generously, to entertain them. Soon, in her grand stuccoed mansion built in the Nash Italianate style and set away from the road at the end of a drive with a huge, umbrageous garden behind it, she gathered aspiring painters and writers as well as others already famous. Family reminiscences describe them – Hunt, Millais, Brett, the Rossettis; sometimes also Thomas Carlyle, Ruskin, and Tennyson, discussing the latest pictures and books, sharing round each other's letters, drinking wine on the cool lawns or by the fire in the great sitting-room. Its walls were papered in fig-green, the furniture upholstered in crocus-yellow, the colours chosen by Thomas Woolner in daring, fresh Pre-Raphaelite tones – his sculpture 'Love' under a dome, gracing the milky, marble mantel-piece. A sacred chair stood in a corner, once occupied by Ralph Emerson who had talked at length on the gender of deity. Eliza herself played the piano, singing one of Byron's *Hebrew Melodies*, 'She walks in Beauty like the night';[15] Thackeray, perhaps after a snub, unkindly called her a 'jolly fellow'.[16]

Coventry, of course, was there, too; not yet a member of the family but hoping shortly to be one. As soon as he was regularly employed at the British Museum, small though his salary was, he was able to ask Emily to marry him. He did so in May 1847, in the Hampstead fields, as he and the family took a walk close to the ancient parish church. In his poem *The Angel in the House* he described his hero, Felix Vaughan, making such a proposal to Honor, the eldest daughter of the Dean of Salisbury, in a way that was doubtless close to his own.[17]

> I grew assured, before I ask'd,
>   That she'd be mine without reserve,
> And in her unclaim'd graces bask'd,
>   At leisure, till the time should serve,
>
> Till once, through lanes returning late,
>   Her laughing sisters lagg'd behind;
> And, ere we reach'd her father's gate,
>   We paused with one presentient mind;
> And, in the dim and perfumed mist,
>   Their coming stay'd, who, blythe and free,
> And very woman, loved to assist
>   A lover's opportunity.
>
> Twice rose, twice died my trembling word:
>   The faint and frail Cathedral chimes
> Spake time in music, and we heard
>   The chafers rustling in the limes.
>
> Her dress, that touch'd me where I stood;
>   The warmth of her confided arm;
> Her bosom's gentle neighbourhood;
>   Her pleasure in her power to charm;
> Her look, her love, her form, her touch,
>   The least seem'd most by blissful turn,
> Blissful but that it pleased too much,
>   And taught the wayward soul to yearn.
> It was as if a harp with wires
>   Was traversed by the breath I drew;
> And, oh, sweet meeting of desires,
>   She, answering, own'd that she loved too.

The marriage took place three months later at St John's Hampstead, on September 11th, witnessed by Charles and Eliza Orme, and Coventry's mother, Eliza Patmore.[18] The couple went to

Hastings for the honeymoon, a town Coventry had known since childhood, a resort still without the railway, remote, peaceful and quite unspoilt, a day's journey from London by coach.

In *The Angel in the House* Coventry described it, although in the names of Felix and Honor: how they boated and paddled and shopped; how they passed their happy evenings; how they found it all such fun.[19]

> So we two wore our strange estate:
>   Familiar, unaffected, free,
> We talk'd, until the dusk grew late,
>   Of this and that; but, after tea,
> As doubtful if a lot so sweet
>   As our's was our's in very sooth,
> Like children, to promote conceit,
>   We feign'd that it was not the truth;
> And she assumed the maiden coy,
>   And I adored remorseless charms,
> And then we clapp'd our hands for joy,
>   And ran into each other's arms.

In Emily's arms Coventry found a transcendental joy of a kind quite beyond anything he had imagined. All his work for the rest of his life was inspired by it. For the moment, however, all thoughts of poetry were laid aside. The weather was superb, the thermometer touched the seventies. There was Batty's circus and the celebrated Distin family playing the sax-horns and sax-tubas; while, for the more serious there was a lecture by Mrs Balfour on 'The Moral and intellectual influence of Women on Society'. The whole honeymoon was marvellous. It was, as the local newspaper said of Mrs Balfour's lecture, 'plain, simple, chaste – a treat of no common kind.'[20]

CHAPTER FIVE

Family Life and Literary Friendships

P ETER GEORGE'S literary friends were not the only members of the public to read Coventry's first poems and think them full of interest and promise. Thanks to several good reviews, quite a number of people bought them, many of whom were poets themselves. Amongst these was Thomas Woolner, a talented sculptor. He admired Coventry's work enormously and soon met him, visiting the Ormes when Coventry was there courting Emily. Woolner was already in sight of success and had joined the circle of writers and artists who were always welcomed at Avenue Road. He was shortly to be a Pre-Raphaelite, one of the original seven Brethren of whom the leader was Dante Gabriel Rossetti. Rossetti, too, knew Coventry's poems, having read a review and ordered them, telling his brother he thought them 'stunning'. Soon Coventry became intimate with all the other members of the group: with Hunt, Stephens, Millais and Collinson. Older than they were by several years, already almost a public figure, he received their cheerful, youthful homage, being classed as one of the 'Immortals' along with Tennyson and Robert Browning, although strangely nicknamed 'The Vampire'. His work was felt to be like their own, individual and true to nature. 'The best one can hope as a painter just now,' D. G. Rossetti wrote to him, 'is to have a place of some kind among those who are to do for painting, as far as possible, what you and a very few more poets are doing now for poetry.'[1]

His close links with the Pre-Raphaelites opened before him a new world in which he is almost better known by students of that particular period than he is for his *Angel in the House*. He wrote in *The Germ*, the Brotherhood's magazine, which only survived for two issues but which still remains of literary interest; his profile was sculpted in plaster by Woolner for one of the latter's successful medallions; a scene from his poem 'The Woodman's Daughter' was painted by Millais and hung in the Royal Academy. He even became the means of recruiting the greatest champion of the movement. John Ruskin was then a critic of the utmost influence. Thanks to Coventry's marriage to Emily, who had known Ruskin since her childhood, Coventry, too, shared his friendship. When the Brethren needed help in the face of withering attacks in the press, Coventry asked him to come to their aid. Ruskin gave them vigorous support in two long letters to *The Times*. Coventry himself was directly implicated in attacks on the Pre-Raphaelites. Millais' painting of *The Woodman's Daughter* acknowledged Coventry's authorship beneath it. Deliberately mis-printing his poem, abusing him as well as the Brethren, the *Art Journal*, for instance, had written, 'With respect to the subject, it is supplied by a verse of a poet named Coventry Patmore. These young men may form a world of their own in Art, but the prestige of even their eccentricity cannot be sustained by their verse.'[2]

Coventry's closest link was made with Woolner. As early as 1849, even before the formation of the Brotherhood, he had given Coventry a cast of his 'Puck' for which Coventry thanked him warmly, still writing in formal terms.[3] 'My Dear Sir', Coventry wrote on the 20th April,

Pray receive my best thanks for your 'Puck'. I know that I am not a competent judge of its merits, but I know also that it gives me very true pleasure, entirely apart from the pleasure it gives me as the gift of so sincere an admirer of my own efforts in art . . . I feel confident that your work will grow upon me: I write late at night, and I like it now three times as much as I did at the beginning of the evening – and I liked it then.

Their acquaintance soon warmed to friendship. As often happens amongst artists, who like to use their friends as models, having finished Coventry's likeness, Woolner decided to sculpt Emily. This portrait remains in the family, a fine example of his early work in plaster.

'The more I look at the medallion of my wife, the more I admire it and the more I feel the great obligation you have put me under, in doing it,' Coventry told him in October 1850.[4]

The children of Coventry and Emily Patmore

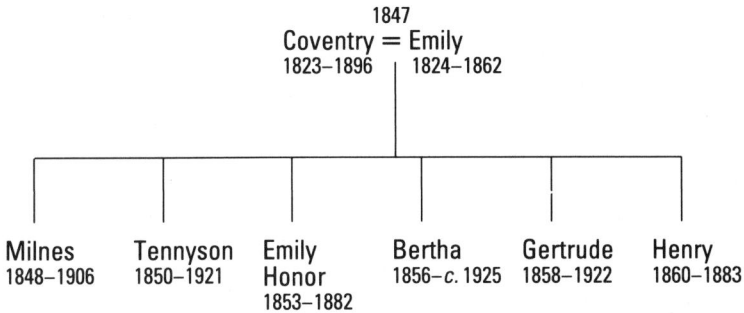

```
                          1847
                  Coventry = Emily
                  1823–1896 | 1824–1862
                            |
     ┌──────────┬──────────┬──────────┬──────────┬──────────┐
  Milnes     Tennyson    Emily       Bertha    Gertrude    Henry
 1848–1906   1850–1921   Honor     1856–c.1925 1858–1922  1860–1883
                         1853–1882
```

He enclosed, too, in the same letter a poem Woolner had sent him for criticism. 'I return your poem which seems to me to have been greatly improved by your alterations. It is now a very sweet and pure piece of verse . . . I hope you are not going to stick this pretty flower in the dung-heap of *The Leader*.' Their friendship lasted throughout their lives, including Emily warmly within it. In the summer of 1854 Woolner wrote to her from Australia where for a time he had gone to work. In reply, Emily told him,[5]

It gave me very great pleasure to hear from you. I knew the writing in a moment, and though I had just returned hungry from a long walk, and there was a lobster and beer on the table, I read every word of your letter before I tasted a morsel!!!

We have all been ill, Coventry, Milnes, my baby, a little girl, born since you left, and named Emily Honoria – and myself. Little Tennyson whom you perhaps remember as the baby with curly golden hair is always well, and is as pretty as can be imagined. We are all well now so I will not tell you of all the illnesses we have had. I will not fall into the mother's fault of describing my own children, but I must tell you that Milnes is as clever as ever, and that the Baby is very pretty.

I feel as if I had written rather a stupid letter. It will not mend the matter to say I have done my best; yet such is the fact, so you must not expect better another time. I have said nothing about yourself but you know how heartily I wish you all good.

If Coventry were here he would join yours most sincerely

E. A. PATMORE

Her two boys to whom she referred, the elder, Milnes, the second, Tennyson, had been given their names for the same reason, to honour and recall their godfathers. When she had given birth to the first in the summer of 1848, Coventry had written to Monckton Milnes.[6]

I wish very much that my little boy should be called by a name which shall remind him of his father's debts to one, but for whose kindness there would have been no little boy to be named. Will you impose upon me an additional obligation to gratitude by conferring upon my son, in your name, a continual lesson of thankfulness? If you are disposed to grant my request, you will be pleased to know that Mrs Procter will be associated with you in this kindness to

Your affectionate friend

COVENTRY K. PATMORE

Like Thomas Woolner, Monckton Milnes remained a true friend for life in spite of a busy public career and innumerable demanding attachments in every artistic field. He was, if anything, more a godfather to Coventry than he was to the little boy he sponsored, giving him help in financial crises as well as comfort in times of disaster. Coventry was always deeply grateful. Although he found it hard to say so, being shy and extremely reserved, he opened his heart when writing letters. Thanks to a recommendation of Milnes to a Parliamentary Commission of Inquiry, Coventry and other staff at the British Museum had been given better security and salaries in the summer of 1851. Coventry wrote on this occasion,[7]

You will be pleased to hear that, among other steps which have been taken by the Trustees of the Museum, at the suggestion of the Commission, they have very considerably improved the position of the 'supernumerary assistants', of whom, for five years, I have been one, at a salary of (practically) about £120. The whole class is now *permanent*. The income, on entering, is £130, with an increase of £10 each year for seven years, back service being allowed for: so that my income, after this quarter is £180, and in two years hence it will be £200 – which seems

Coventry Patmore, aged 32.
Drawing by John Brett

Emily Patmore, aged 30.
Wash drawing by John Brett

Dr. Edward Andrews,
Emily's father, aged 37.
(Item 3 in Appendix B)

Elizabeth Andrews,
Emily's mother, c. 1812.
Miniature by an unknown artist

Emily Patmore, aged 26.
Sculpted medallion
by Thomas Woolner

Beresford Chapel, Walworth, in 1824. Watercolour by J. Hassell
Beresford Chapel: the interior in 1825. Watercolour by J. Yates

Dr. Andrews, aged 33.
The popular preacher,
a glamorised print.
(Item 2 in Appendix B)

Peter George Patmore,
Coventry's father.
Self-portrait, undated

Emily Patmore, aged 35.
Oil painting by John Brett

Eliza Orme, Emily's eldest sister with
whom she lived after the death of her
father. Oil painting, artist and date
unrecorded

Emily Patmore. Collodion positive photograph, undated. Photographer unknown

North End, Hampstead, from the Heath. Elm Cottage, in which Emily died, is the tallest of the three houses seen in the background. Print from drawing by G. Childs, c. 1840

"THE ANGEL IN 'THE HOUSE;'" OR, THE RESULT OF FEMALE SUFFRAGE.
(*A Troubled Dream of the Future.*)

Coventry Patmore, aged 71. Oil painting by J. S. Sargent

to me to be very fair pay for the ordinary business of the Library. There is only one thing that makes me discontented, and that is, that I do not think you well know how happy and really well-off I am, mainly through your goodness. I long for you to come and see us some day – not for half an hour but for an afternoon or evening. I know that this is hoping for a great deal; but you have justified me amply in believing that your interest in my affairs is enough to make you take pleasure in becoming an eye-witness of their prosperity.

Believe me, ever affectionately yours,

COVENTRY K. PATMORE

The year before, on September 3rd 1850, he had also written 'Ever affectionately yours' to Milnes, with general news on this occasion, in a letter which shows how close he felt towards him. It shines a warm light on their friendship, and gives a little picture, too, of his social life and literary activities.[8]

I did not write to you at Marienbad because, during the month named by you for your stay there I had no account to render of improved health. My wife's confinement delayed my departure from London so long that I am but just returned from spending my holiday with the Tennysons, at Coniston Water. I am now strong and well again, and hope, by observing temperance in work, and being careful in all other respects, to keep off illness for the future.

I was very much pleased with Mrs Tennyson. She seems to be just the right woman to suit her husband. She is evidently entirely devoted to him. They are staying now in a house lent to them by Mrs Marshall; and do not seem to have yet determined anything as to their place of permanent abode.

A *fourth* edition of two thousand copies of *In Memoriam* is preparing. This, I suppose, is the quickest sale of poetry since Lord Byron's time.

You will be pleased to hear that I have a good prospect of having a long Paper in the *Edinburgh Review* in the beginning of next year – but this is a secret.

Coventry's interest in *In Memoriam* was more than that of simply another writer, pleased to note the success of a friend. He had a personal pride in it, having, in fact, saved it from the dustbin. Tennyson had left it behind in a cupboard, and Coventry had found it just in time. He often used to speak of this, and one of his friends, William Allingham, who was himself a

budding poet of just Coventry's own age, recorded the story in
his diary.

Like many of Coventry's early friends, Allingham had read his
first poems and taken the trouble to get in touch with him. They
met in the British Museum Library for which Patmore had sent
him a ticket, and immediately felt a mutual sympathy. Coventry
asked him home for supper. They walked back to Camden
Town to 10 Cambridge Villas. This is how Allingham described
it.[9]

Neat small house on left-hand side of road, near a railway bridge.
Mrs Patmore – 'Emily'. Tea and cake. Two small sitting-rooms with
folding door between: front room has engraved portraits of Wordsworth and Faraday over the mantelpiece ('the two greatest men of our
time'), a round table with ten or a dozen books, and a plaster cast of a
statuette of Puck – just alighted on a mushroom . . . A very original bit
of work, by 'a young artist named Woolner'. In the back room P.'s
writing-table at the window, with a few bookshelves beside it . . . Then
we started on a walk northward . . . We came to Hampstead Heath. The
evening was growing cold as we returned to Highgate and descended
the hill, P. showing me on the way the house, in a sort of crescent with
trees before it, where he formerly lived, and where Emerson and
Tennyson sat at his table and liked each other. After some supper
Patmore said . . . 'I have in this room perhaps the greatest literary
treasure in England – the mansuscript of Tennyson's *next poem*. It is
written in a thing like a butcher's account-book. He left it behind him in
his lodging when he was up in London and wrote to me to go and look
for it. He had no other copy, and he never remembers his verses. I
found it by chance, in a drawer; if I had been a little later it would
probably have been sold to a butter shop.' . . . I was not even told the
title at this time. It was *In Memoriam*. 'It is the best thing he has ever
done,' said Patmore.

Coventry's rescue of *In Memoriam* sealed a friendship with
Alfred Tennyson, begun at a party given by the Procters, which
gave his second son a godfather, lasted until Emily's death, and
only then came to an end by accident. As with others like Milnes
and Allingham, Tennyson had read his early poems, had praised
them generously when they met, and even suggested, according
to Coventry, that some might one day surpass his own. Tenny-

son was older by fourteen years, already famous, soon to be Laureate. His prophecies went to Coventry's head. For many months Coventry worshipped him, seeing him almost every day, walking with him for hours in the evenings, constantly asking him home to dinner. Tennyson liked him and so put up with it, although sometimes his patience waned and he humbled Coventry with snubs and silences. On one occasion when asked to Camden to meet a number of Coventry's friends he came and refused to speak at all. He could, however, be very companionable. 'My dear P.,' he wrote one morning in an undated note. 'Dine with me today at 6 o cl if you can. I have a fowl & a bottle of sherry. I leave this at your gates. Ever yours A T.'[10] He was kind, too, to Coventry's friends, even when they were not distinguished. Allingham found him at his best when he went to call at Coventry's instance. Again, he recorded it all in his diary,[11]

. . . in the summer of 1851 Coventry Patmore, to my boundless joy, let me know that I might call on the great Poet, then not long married, and living at Twickenham.

I was admitted, shown upstairs into a room with books lying about, and soon came in a tall, broad-shouldered swarthy man, slightly stooping, with loose dark hair and beard. He wore spectacles, and was obviously very near-sighted. Hollow cheeks and the dark pallor of his skin gave him an unhealthy appearance. He was a strange and almost spectral figure. The Great Man peered close at me, and then shook hands cordially, yet with a profound quietude of manner. He was then about forty-one, but looked much older, from his bulk, his short-sight, stooping shoulders, and loose careless dress. He looked tired, and said he had been asleep and was suffering from hay-fever. Mrs Tennyson came in, very sweet and courteous, with low soft voice, and by and by when I rose to take leave she said, 'Won't you stay for dinner?'

After tea he went upstairs and smoked, Patmore and I sitting with him . . . When we took leave T. came out to the gate and again shook hands with me . . . We walked to Richmond railway station, I feeling that a longing of my life had been fulfilled, and as if I had been familiar for years with this great and simple man.

This summer of Allingham's visit, the year of Millais' *The Woodman's Daughter* and Ruskin's defence of the Pre-Raphaelites, opened for both Coventry and Emily the happiest time of their marriage. They had moved from Camden up to Highgate to a quiet street known as The Grove, a leafy terrace which still exists, lined with brick and stucco cottages, on the very edge of Hampstead Heath. Here, on every fourth weekend, friends gathered for tea and supper to walk, talk and be cosy with Emily. She was the one that everyone liked. Many were fond of Coventry, too; but some found him a literary snob and had their reservations.

The arrangements for getting people together in their new house, so far away, proved a little complicated. At first they had been 'at home' fortnightly. Then, as Emily wrote to William Rossetti, on 22nd January, 1851,[12]

As we find our alternate Saturday meetings are somewhat thinly attended, the last only having brought us one visitor, and that before, none at all, we propose changing them to *monthly* meetings, and fixing the first Saturday of each month for them. We shall by this means, be likely to see a larger number of our friends each time, and Mr. Patmore, who is now extremely busy will gain an evening.

[The new plan proved a success, and all sorts of people came to them. Writing again to William Rossetti, Emily asked him] Will you and your brother take tea with us next Thursday evening at eight o'clock? We are expecting a young lady who is very susceptible to mesmerism, upon whom you might try your power as a mesmerist. Mr. Patmore succeeded by making only six or eight passes, and even made her slightly clairvoyante.

It is a long while since I have seen your brother. I hope he will arrange to come. I will show him original poems by Mr. & Mrs Browning in my scrapbook.

They stayed at The Grove for six years until, under financial pressure, they decided to let their house and move. They went north to Fortis Green. 'Could you look in and have tea with us on Sunday at seven?' Coventry wrote to the same correspondent. 'We are on the point of taking our final departure from The Grove for the inaccessible wilds of Finchley.'[13] They had tried a move once before, about which there is some correspondence. Coventry had explained to Allingham:[14]

I have resolved – and may I have heart to persevere – utterly to cut 'our periodical literature' as being altogether a base and unsatisfactory way of expending one's energies and earning one's tin. This vow cuts off half my income, but in order to fulfil it, I have dropped both my servants and taken lodgings at Hendon for my wife and children, where we can get wholesome food, shelter, and a pew at church, on two hundred a year. For the first time in the last ten years I have now health of mind and body and *conscience* to write poetry, which I propose to do henceforward according to the capacity I have been made with.

Emily, forced to take the strain with three children and no servants, for once came out with a little complaint. 'Sometimes I almost wish that something would interfere with our letting the house after all,' she wrote to Coventry who had gone to Hastings. 'Nothing but the recollection of your Poem makes me reasonable again. Indeed, you ought to work very hard when your wife makes such a great sacrifice for the sake of enabling you to do it. You have almost reason to be jealous of the Poem when you find I will give you up for it.'[15] As it proved, her wish was granted. No one was found to rent their house, and after a month they went back to it.

The temporary loss of two servants meant more to Emily than extra work. She particularly liked the companionship of staff and felt a genuine and deep compassion for the little maids who came to The Grove, to whom a comfortable bed was a dream. She took immense trouble to train them to better themselves for future employment. When she finally left The Grove she decided to write a book to help them.

This she did in 1859, under the pen-name of 'Mrs Motherly', and called it *The Servants' Behaviour Book*, 'Hints on Manners and Dress for maid servants in small households'.

Its interest lies for the reader today in the work she expected her girls to do and the way in which she taught them to do it. Mainly, of course, it was cleaning and washing, but also waiting and serving at the table. When there were guests the meals were elaborate, with soup, fish, meat and poultry, followed by fruit, tarts and cheeses; wine in decanters, beer in jugs and plain water in special bottles on each of which was placed a glass. The table was laid with mathematical care, and the meal progressed according to rules which the girls, clearly, found mystifying.

Everything had to be handed round. Novice parlour-maids must have been terrified. Emily soothed them as best she could. 'Let every girl remember,' she assured them in her book, 'that a simple dinner, with good waiting, will always appear more hospitable, and be more comfortable, than a costly one, with bad waiting . . . It is better to be slow, than to spill gravy, overturn glasses, catch your foot in chair legs, let things fall, or make noises with knocking china and glass. I must warn you against smiling at droll stories told at table,' she concluded, for above all, a servant must not make her presence felt or be 'seeming in anyway to notice or enter into the conversation.'[16]

Coventry was a good story-teller, as were many of his friends. At times there must have been much hilarity and Emily probably wrote her warning after embarassing personal experience when her stern glare had failed to attract the notice of the girls, waiting meekly to clear away, as they listened-in to a comic tale or even joined a general burst of laughter. Many people who came to The Grove to these carefully arranged dinners must have admired Emily's efforts and the brave smile that lit her face as beer frothed on the best tablecloth, vegetables toppled onto the carpet, and the guests' chairs were jarred by the maids' kicks. The star was frequently Alfred Tennyson; Ruskin often came too, as did Millais and both the Brownings.

In the neighbouring small sitting-room to which they adjourned after the meal, the air was one of cosy taste, with chairs covered in comfortable velvet, tables strewn with selected books, and prints and pictures on the walls, one of which had been done by Millais. It showed Emily full-face with her hair widely bunched at the sides. Coventry told the artist, John Brett, that 'he hated Millais' portrait of his wife beyond speech.'[17] He felt obliged to tell Millais that he liked it, however. Millais, thanking him, wrote on the 22nd October, 1851, 'I was delighted to hear of your full satisfaction at Mrs Patmore's portrait.'[18] Robert Browning depicted her better:

> If one could have that little head of hers
>   Painted upon a background of pale gold,
> Such as the Tuscan's early art prefers!

This is from a poem of twenty-two lines in all, which he published later in *Dramatis Personae* under the title of 'A Face'. The best likenesses were done by Brett whose swift sketches in pencil and ink surely caught her charm exactly. He also did a portrait in oils which Coventry liked. It was much admired and later hung and praised in the Royal Academy.

John Brett was a friend of the Ormes through whom he probably met the Patmores. He came to love Emily dearly, as many entries in his journal showed.[19] 'Saw Mrs P. & had a long and agreeable chat . . .' he noted in October, 1852. '. . . after tea walked to Kentish Town to call on Patmore. Saw him and Mrs P. & Millais' Portrait & enjoyed the visit & read a MSS poem of his about to be published.' '. . . last Saty evening I spent at (Patmore's) house, being invited to meet Holman Hunt . . .' Also he met Millais there. Both impressed him tremendously. 'I am going fast towards pre-raphaelitism,' he confided in May, 1853, 'Millais & Hunt are truly fine fellows. I greatly admire them & honor them. I have resolved in future to go through a severe course of training & close child-like study of nature . . . in short to follow in their steps.'

His work began to bear their mark, especially 'The Hedger' of 1860 below which was a verse by Coventry.[20]

> In dim recesses hyacinths drooped,
> And breadths of primrose lit the air.

He gave his host his respect as a poet but as a man he disliked him cordially. He thought his 'deportment' was 'super cold & repelling'.[21] When he paid a visit to The Grove, as was the case with many of his friends, the person he went to see was darling Emily.

Browning described her with lips parted as though on the point of kissing a flower, and this was a characteristic attitude. Brett painted her like this, too. It gave her an air of expectant pleasure which everyone found unusual and charming. Above her mouth was a prominent nose and great, clear, hazel eyes, capped with a mass of dark hair which, at parties, she bound up but which, informally, hung in ringlets. Tennyson thought her 'a perfect woman . . . of enchanting innocence and simplicity of manner . . .'[22] Another poet, Aubrey de Vere, recorded her 'beauty and high abilities.'[23] Richard Garnett, Coventry's colleague at the British Museum, spoke of her 'beauty, talents and accomplishments . . .' her 'queenly dignity . . . gentleness, humility'.[24] In build she was a little plump, what her family called 'a Juno figure'. As to height she was not very tall. She had to stand on the tips of her toes if she wished her often parted lips to reach Coventry's passive face, to touch his own to kiss them.

Coventry's normally arrogant air, his 'haughty manner' as Emily called it, which Brett and others so disliked, concealed an inner warmth and passion which was only allowed to appear in very dilute form, even amongst their intimate friends. However much he played the part of the lofty, poetic intellectual, preserving dignity at all times; and however much before the public, Emily behaved with wifely submission, it is quite clear that on their own they behaved like a normal, cheerful couple who, at heart, were deeply in love.

A glimpse of this may be seen in their letters, heavily censored though they were before they were printed in Champneys' biography. A year after their marriage he wrote,[25]

Let us crown all our blessings by feeling grateful to God for them. What could we have prayed for that we have not? We are married and love completely: we have a sweet little outward symbol of our union: St. Paul's prayer that we should have neither riches nor poverty has been ours, and it has been granted: that we may not be narrow and selfish in our bliss, a friend* has been given us, whom we have every reason to think echoes our devotion to him not faintly; so that our circle of love is complete . . .

Oh! how I long for Monday afternoon, when I shall come *home* and find the house with the spirit in it that makes it home . . . In all you do you are like an angel in Heaven, where, as Dante says 'everything is done zealously and well.'[26]

I tremble in mind when I think of the fortune which I enjoy . . . The most noble and lovely of women for my wife: three of the prettiest children ever seen: health made delightful by preceding years of languor, and, hard at hand, worldly honour and prosperity; and, almost

* Tennyson

above all, the assured feeling of being called to do a work which, to him who can do it, must necessarily be the greatest of delights as well as the greatest of duties.[27]

All that I have written in the 'Angel' about love is much below the intensity and delicacy of the plain reality.[28]

Emily's replies were equally tender. At the seaside, after an illness, she compared herself to a hermit crab which she found on the beach, out of its shell.[29]

Can you fancy how naked, cold, homeless, and imperfect it must have felt, and how it must have longed for the warm, safe shell again? This is exactly how I feel. I have crawled out of my shell and am longing with all my might to be safe in it again. This is exactly how I always know I shall feel, to my life's end, if you die first. I cannot tell you how exactly it expresses the feeling I have when you are away – the weak, unsafe, unconcentrated feeling . . .

It requires separation to keep up the mere romance of love . . . I daresay we shall find through our whole lives that we shall fancy the romance is gone whenever we have been together for twelve months; whereas a week's parting will bring it back directly, however old we may be. I can quite well imagine you kissing a long grey hair when I was away nursing a grandchild. If only we can be good Christians we must go on loving each other more and more.[30]

When she was ill, friends supported them. Coventry wrote, 'I had a letter from Brett insisting on your seeing Dr Kidd, and saying that, as money could be our only objection, he also insisted on paying a fee for him to go down to see you: accordingly he enclosed £20. Just think of the poor young painter's devotion to you. He will be my dearest friend to the end of my life.'[31]

Coventry's appearance has been preserved in a careful drawing by John Brett which shows him staring thoughtfully downwards, his pale face and dark hair, which is brushed in softly poetic waves, giving him a pensive, calm expression. Perhaps he was thinking about his poem which at the time had just come out, the first volume of *The Angel in the House*. He had spent years searching for a theme by which he could honour his love for Emily. 'I have been meditating a poem for you;' he had written to her, even before they were married, 'but I am determined not to give you anything I write unless it is the best thing I have ever written. O, how much the best it ought to be, if it would do justice to its subject.'[32]

At last, inspiration came to him, the magic moment when all was clear. Perhaps he was on a country walk, as described in the *Angel's* Prologue, when he realised he had hit on a plan that exactly fitted his aspirations – how he could write a poem on love that was more than a simple romantic idyll, but something deeper and more realistic.

> And, in a loftier phrase, he talk'd
>   With her upon their Wedding-Day,
> While thro' the new-mown meads they walk'd,
>   Their children shouting by the way:
> 'Not careless of the gift of song,
>   'Nor out of love with noble fame,
> 'I, meditating much and long
>   'What I should sing, how win a name,
> 'In green and undiscover'd ground,
>   'Yet near where many others sing,
> 'I have the very well-head found
>   'Whence gushes the Pierian Spring.'
> Then she: 'What is it, Dear? The Life
>   'Of Arthur, or Jerusalem's Fall?'
>   'Neither: your gentle self, my wife,
>   'Yourself, and love that's all in all.'

For this, his happy marriage had prepared him. Further, the time was exactly right for such a poem to please the public. One of the burning topics of the day was the role of the wife in modern society – whether to follow her husband meekly or to insist on equal partnership. Coventry wrote in favour of the former, seeing in Emily's obedient love a deeply religious, moving simile, that of the soul as the bride of Christ. But fate took *The Angel* out of his hands. Instead of remaining a narrative poem about a pious, loving couple, it became a kind of manual of matrimony. The title itself became a catch-phrase which entered into the English language. To be an 'Angel in the House' acquired its own particular meaning, that of a perfect, docile spouse. Its author became, quite by chance, something he never wished to be, the spokesman of pure, connubial love. As he sadly came to realise, after reading a *Saturday Review* in which his name was held to ridicule, he found himself, against his will, a kind of father-confessor of Love.[33] He was singled out as the arch-priest of the Darby-and-Joan reformed religion and accused of providing a golden calf; a household god for artless couples to worship in every home.

CHAPTER SIX

An Angel's Place is in the Home

THE STATUS of women (in the 19th century variously described as 'the woman's sphere', 'the woman's role', 'the position of woman') had, when Coventry wrote *The Angel*, changed little since the Middle Ages, certainly since the 14th century and the reign of Henry IV. It was still governed by common law in which, on marriage, the woman's identity ceased to exist in practical terms. All her property became her husband's; her very presence merged with his so that, in law, they were one person, *unica persona, quia caro una et sanguis unus*. The woman thus had no redress for any hurt she suffered from her husband, whether legal, moral or physical. It was held in law to be self-inflicted because she and her husband were one. In all but name she became a slave from the very moment she left the church to become, as the saying had it, happily married.

This injustice, so long endured, was challenged in the 19th century for various interesting reasons. The wealth of the Industrial Revolution greatly increased the population, in particular the middle class, and especially the female sex, which previously had been diminished by the ever recurring danger of childbed. Thus by 1851, the year of the sixth decennial census, women were found to outnumber men by 860,000. Women also had more leisure than ever they had enjoyed before – women, that is, of the middle class – finding plenty of servants to help them, and being able to buy in shops a thousand items made by machinery which, before, they had made themselves. So, with extra time to spare, they began to think about self-improvement. This led to better education, if not for themselves, at least for their daughters. In the minds of the more intelligent were sown the seeds of emancipation; and dreams were dreamt of socialist schemes for Liberty, Equality, and Sorority.

There were plenty of books to help them do so. From about the time of Victoria's accession in 1837, itself a milestone in feminist progress, numerous volumes began to appear in which the feminist cause was advanced. This, of course, produced a reaction, so that many others came into print which praised the woman's traditional role. These proved an enormous success, especially those by Mrs Ellis, whose *Women of England, Mothers of England, Daughters of England, Wives of England*, were sold out and reprinted again and again for more than a decade; the last was dedicated to Queen Victoria.

The ideas in these books had the support of a generation, the mothers of Mrs Ellis's 'Daughters', who had grown up in another age when public morality was not so strict, who were now ashamed of their former tolerance towards adultery and irreligion. Added to which they were blessed by the Church, quickened from its 18th-century sloth by the fires of the Evangelical Revival and the Tractarian Movement. The marriage vow again was sacred. The feminist wish for cohabitation, based on mutual love alone, and to be dissolved when love had passed, as preached by the more Utopian socialists like Godwin, Shelley and Robert Owen, was considered to be a temptation of the Devil. The Gothic Revival helped this reaction, too. To think of a woman as a Queen of Beauty, presiding over a knightly tournament, was much easier and more fun than it was to imagine her sitting in parliament, presiding over a difficult debate. For feminists wanted the franchise as well as matrimonial reform. Thus from three points of view – the moral, the religious and the stylistic – the movement to alter women's status found the spirit of the times against it.

In February, 1851, in a long survey of two books by three prominent women reformers published in the *North British Review*, Coventry marshalled the arguments against feminism with vigour and intellectual clarity.[1] He began by reviewing the current arguments in words that left no doubt at all as to where his sympathies lay: as he put it, with, 'The woman's excellent privilege of subordination, and the man's ennobling responsibility as chief'. Quite obviously a woman's status, vis-à-vis her place in Heaven, was equal in every respect to the man's. Equally obviously, here on Earth, her natural place was behind her husband.

The social subordination of woman to man is a law of nature: it is not a thing that can ever be reasonably called into question. That men have the strongest muscles no one doubts . . . This being the case – the social subordination of women [is] an irreversible natural law . . . [On the other hand, he continued,] The self-dependence which should be allowed to woman, is based on the ground of her being a spiritual agent born with man under a common moral law, and with a common hope of immortality.

As he put it poetically, 'his sweet coheiress of immortal life.' He developed his theme with conventional arguments, mocking the women who wore trousers or 'bloomers' and those who attacked conventional female dress with its cage-like hoops or crinolines. He blamed it all on the infidel French: 'It was among the fetid and gaudy poppies which dyed the harvest of the first French Revolution, that the doctrine of the "equality" of man and woman first, in modern times, arose . . . To a wide moral debasement, therefore, it is that we refer the present revival of this ridiculous question.' Fortunately, he and his readers were British; and he went on to 'confirm and clarify the knowledge of the truth, which, with hearty gratitude to God, we perceive to prevail, although somewhat dimmed and confused, in the breasts of most of those who have been nurtured in this favoured island.'

Here Coventry touched on a subject very close to the national heart. This was the cult of 'home sweet home'. There the woman reigned; and Coventry drew a romantic picture of a home life, perhaps his own, in which the wife with 'Christian meekness' gave her lord a cup of tea, thus restoring his 'nervous system' after a gruelling day at the office. He ended up with a wise conclusion: that the woman's position would never improve until the man's was better, too, and he had refined his own character. With the help of Christianity, he must first become as good and pure and meek as he himself would like his wife to be.

At the same time as he wrote this article, a dramatic event had taken place in the history of women's suffrage. This had happened in the House of Lords with the lodging of a petition. The first of its kind in the history of the movement, it prayed their Lordships 'to take into their serious Consideration the Propriety of enacting an Electoral Law which will include adult females within its provision.' It was 'presented, read, and Ordered to lie on the Table, and to be received as the Petition of *Mrs Abiah Higginbottom*.' Their Lordships heard it with much amusement, especially pleased with the name of the petitioner. The *Times'* correspondent heard it too, and noted what the Clerk did not, in the daily record in the Lords' Journal: that when their Lordships rose to adjourn, the Chamber rang with aristocratic laughter.[2]

Those who supported women's rights, naturally took it much more seriously. Amongst these was John Stuart Mill, one of the country's leading philosophers, who had long espoused the cause of feminism. He decided to use the Lords' petition as an excuse to write an article in which he discussed the subject generally, including its progress in America where, the summer before, there had been a Women's Rights Convention. He published his thoughts in the *Westminster Review* in a learned essay of thirty-six pages.[3] First of all he marshalled the arguments of all those who derided feminism, and then he demolished them systematically. He said, in summary, 'The strength of the cause lies in the support of those who are influenced by reason and principle . . . There is no difficulty in understanding why the subjection of women has been a custom. No other explanation is needed than physical force.'

If this was clear, as it obviously was, to all those who supported the movement, it was equally clear to all their opponents that Mill's so-called reason and principle was nothing more than declamatory rubbish, not worth serious debate, easily destroyed by simple ridicule.

Liberated women were an easy target. Cartoonists and punsters enjoyed a field-day; *Punch* as usual was in the van. The whole of the subsequent *Punch's Almanack* for 1853 was given over to jokes on women taking the places of men in public. The longest satire was written by 'Jane', a young woman in green spectacles, brought up to be Strong-Minded, whose chief pleasure was going to lectures on all sorts of interesting 'ologies'. At one, in the Royal Institution, she met 'Edward', her future husband, with whom she hoped for a chemical marriage. Once the knot was tied, however, she found he yawned and sauntered off whenever she started a conversation. So she was lonely and very unhappy. At last, in a dream, she found the remedy. She imagined they had their roles reversed, but far from having an amusing time, she suffered a series of horrid shocks. She was first insulted, mounting an omnibus, then frightened in a street commotion, next, dunned for her husband's debts, then bored as she went with him to help him make his choice at the hatters. Last she called on her Member of Parliament, naturally a woman, a Mrs Boroughby, whom she found at home, at work. Mrs Boroughby refused to see her, being absorbed in writing a speech, her home in a state of total confusion. Of course, to complete the joke, Mrs B. was attached to the Home Office, and much too busy for domestic duties. 'Jane' finally realised the truth, that the old ways remained the best. So she achieved a happy marriage, and closed her piece in cheerful support of all those who defended the *status quo*.

And so my dream went on. Everywhere I found that when women attempted men's work, they proved their own unfitness for it – discovered that our notions of the happiness, and freedom, and dignity of the other sex are founded on a mistake, and that it only depends on us to make them our slaves and adorers ...

I saw that the question between the sexes was not one of superiority or inferiority; that our two spheres lay apart from each other, but that each exercised on the other a most blessed influence – man's sphere, the world; woman's sphere, the home ... And I felt that if we are to compare these two spheres, the woman's, – while the narrower – is, in many respects, the nobler of the two, and her part in the battle of life not unfrequently the more important and dangerous one.

This was the lesson of my dream ... and I don't believe I have any 'mission' that can take me away from my own fireside.

'Jane's' concept of the two spheres – the man's in the world and the woman's in the home – represented the main defence of all those who shared her view (the great majority of the middle class) against which the feminist protest was very nearly useless. By the 1850s, the home itself had become a cult; supported by

Church, State and Queen, it represented British life. To build a home was to build a realm. To honour the guardian of both was to honour a woman. A visit to the Great Exhibition, in the summer of 1851, provided proof like nothing else of the importance of the home. Thousands of useful items, 'in every material, in great variety, of the newest and most recherché patterns,' revealed the British skill and taste for domestic order, design and comfort, beyond the foreigner's wildest dreams. The privacy and piety of home life as depicted in novels and magazines gave an equally wondrous impression. It was often said, and widely believed, that the British home like the British Isles had been especially blessed by God as a guiding star for other nations. What more could a woman want than to be in charge of such an establishment? The domestic joy of the Queen and the Prince was mirrored down to the simplest family. If they were blessed by God, so was the home.

In this year, the *Home Circle*, a magazine for all the family, offered a prize for a homely poem which was won by a boy of sixteen named Brucks, from Plymouth. In it he spoke the final word in an epic that in all ran to nearly five hundred lines.

> Oh, Albion! birthplace of the brave and free!
> Queen of the ocean – guard of liberty!
> (With grateful heart I speak,) oh! how has heaven
> Choice bliss unto *thy* social Circles given!
> There woman – fair in modesty – presides
> And white stol'd virtue ev'ry action guides;
> Extending o'er the State her pow'rful arm,
> To shield her votaries from sin and harm;
> May love mid thy Home Circles ever stand,
> The guardian angel of a much bless'd land;
> From the 'Home Circle' England's grandeur springs,
> Its influence over ev'ry scene it flings;
> And not a land before our own can claim
> The foremost place upon the scroll of fame:
> So may she stand through many a future age,
> Adding fresh lustre to her history's page;
> So may her ensign float upon the breeze,
> Spotless and fair, for untold centuries!

Hail! hallow'd Circle! Circle of our Home,
What glad mementoes at thy mention come
Over the heart!

Such, Circle of domestic joys! thou art,
When love within thy limits sways the heart!

Ah! what do not our Homes to Women owe
The loving partner of our life below?

Against emotions such as these, against articles such as
Coventry's and the jokes of *Punch*, the feminist cause, as yet, was
helpless; even though it was widely discussed, and even though
Woman's Mission, one of the best of the movement's books, to
which 'Jane' had referred with scorn, had already reached a
thirteenth edition.[5] Woman's place was in the home, and the
home, luckily for her, was British. That was all there was to be
said. Coventry summed it up himself in a similarly patriotic
manner at the end of one of the books of *The Angel*, putting the
argument more succinctly than Master Brucks in the *Home
Circle*. If Greece had given the world Beauty and Rome had given
it a Legal System, then England had given it Domesticity.[6]

We, in our day, have better done
This thing or that than anyone;
And who but, still admiring, sees
How excellent for images
Was Greece, for laws how wise was Rome;
But read this Poet, and say if home
And private love did e'er so smile
As in that ancient English Isle!

At that time, in the 1850s, the family home of Coventry and
Emily with their children Milnes, Tennyson and Emily, was still
at 8, The Grove, and here in a state of tranquil happiness,
Coventry at last began the poem on which his thoughts had
dwelt so long, at first entitled simply *The Happy Wedding*. After
so many years reflection, his mind was clear and he wrote
quickly. He had published a few sections before in a volume
inscribed to Monckton Milnes entitled *Tamerton Church Tower*.

He had not realised, then, however, that they might be parts of a longer whole. He composed as fast as he possibly could, and came to the end in six weeks, although in the story he made his hero work for an anniversary year. Then, like his narrator, the poet Vaughan, as he got the book at last from the printers, he proudly showed it off to Emily.

> His purpose with performance crown'd,
>   To her, kind critic, he rehears'd,
> When next their Wedding-Day came round,
>   His leisure's labour, 'Book the First'.[7]

His hero was pictured on a lawn, walking excitedly up and down.[8] Coventry must have done the same in the little garden behind his house. Next, he sent copies to his friends and a few to selected literary editors. After that there was nothing to do except to practise the art of patience. He waited quietly like a lover, and looked every day for a word in the post.

CHAPTER SEVEN

The Poem Greeted with Praise and Sneers

THE STORY set out in Coventry's poem, on which he now awaited a verdict (at least the first part of it – five more were due to follow), was simply one of a young man who falls in love with his Guardian's daughter and, after various rebuffs, at last successfully woos her. As a plot, it was not very strong, but this in itself was not important. Long poems were highly fashionable, and if the verse were well constructed and filled with fresh and fine imagery, there was every chance that the public would like it, however simple and old the basic formula. The tale was a story within a story; the narrator was Vaughan, his hero Felix and his heroine Honor, or sometimes Honoria. She was the eldest of three sisters, the others being Mary and Mildred. They lived in Salisbury Cathedral Close with their father, a widower, the Cathedral Dean.

The narrator begins by describing Felix, back from abroad and down from Cambridge, visiting the Dean on a spring morning, after an absence of six years. He is charmed to find his Guardian well, his daughters unexpectedly attractive.[1]

> No change had touch'd my Guardian. Kind,
> By widowhood more than winters bent,
> And settled in a cheerful mind,
> As still foreboding heaven's content.
> Well might he mourn, from her delay'd!
>
> Was this her eldest, Honor, the prude
> Who would not let me pull the swing;
> Who, kiss'd at Christmas, call'd me rude,
> And sobb'd alone, and would not sing?
> How changed! In shape no more a Grace,
> But Venus: milder than the dove:
> Her mother's air; her Norman face;
> Her large sweet eyes, clear lakes of love.

Mary I knew. In former time
   Ailing and pale, she thought that bliss
Was only for a better clime,
   And, heavenly overmuch, scorn'd this.

   And, what, was this my Mildred, she
To herself and all a sweet surprise?
   My Pet, who romp'd and roll'd a hoop?
I wonder'd where thosee daisy eyes
   Had found their touching curve and droop.

At first, Felix favours Mary, then Mildred, but finally decides for Honor. He calls often, and falls in love with her, enchanted by the way she dresses and how the breeze in the garden reveals her figure.[2]

As, through the flowery mazes sweet,
   Fronting the wind that flutter'd blythe,
And loved her shape, and made her feet
   Bare to their insteps proud and lithe,
She approached, all mildness and young trust;

Honor was no brainless milksop, however. She could read several languages and had stern principles about behaviour. She borrowed Felix's *Tasso* for a train journey, and, at a ball, declined to waltz because it was still considered indelicate. She looked sternly at him when asked to do so, and said she would rather dance a quadrille. Felix was crushed, but later on, at a picnic by Stonehenge, he recovered his self confidence. Honor was nice to him, and looked adorable. Once again, the wind played its part.[3]

As to the breeze a flag unfurls
   My spirit expanded, sweetly embraced
By those same gusts which shook her curls
   And vex'd the ribbon at her waist.
To the future cast I future cares;
   Breathed with a heart unfreighted, free,
And laugh'd at the presumptuous airs
   That with her muslins folded me;

Finally he wins her, and sings for joy like any lover, using popular chivalric jargon.[4]

So Honor was to be my bride!
    The hopeless heights of hope were scaled:

My Queen was crouching at my side,
    By love unsceptered and brought low,
Her awful garb of maiden pride
    All melted into tears like snow.

Her spirit, which I loved to invest
    With pity for my poor desert,
Buried its face within my breast,
    Like a pet fawn by hunters hurt.

Thus ends the first part, entitled *The Betrothal*.

   The poem was set in twelve 'Idylls', interspersed by short pieces, all on the subject of love and women, under the titles of 'Accompaniments' and 'Sentences'. All in all the whole composition filled 191 pages made up of 2114 lines. It made a nice little book, bound in brown cloth, well printed, and published by John Parker of the Strand, who was widely respected. Any critic who picked it up and turned over the leaves would have known, at least, that it ought to be given serious consideration.

   In the event, the reviews were disastrous. The story was felt to be much too slight; the rhymed quatrains repetitive and boring; the accompanying verses between the 'Idylls' difficult to follow and very disruptive. Two of the most powerful voices, *The Times* and *Blackwood*'s, simply ignored it. The *Literary Gazette* thought it might be a joke.[5] 'Were it not for the seriousness of the poem, and the respectability of the publisher, we should regard the whole book as a burlesque, or a mischievous piece of waggery perpetrated on worthy people at Salisbury.' The *Athenaeum* decided to give it four inches under the heading of 'Minor Minstrels'.[6] Worse than this, the critic did so as a parody in rhymed quatrains, quoting some of the feeblest lines so as to show he was not exaggerating; and ending up, 'From ball to bed, from field to farm, The tale flows nicely purling on. With much conceit, there is no harm, In the love-legend here begun. – The rest will come another day if public sympathy allows; – And this is all we have to say, About "The Angel in the House".'

Only one journal gave it serious notice – *The Critic*, on December 1st, 1854, two weeks after it came out. This was a proper full-length review of four columns with plentiful quotations. There could be no doubt that the writer had really liked it and had fully understood what Coventry was trying to say. 'This is an excellent line,' he wrote of a description of maidenly pride in one of the 'Accompaniments'[7] – *Her pleasure in her power to charm* – 'for which the author deserves to be presented with a service of plate from the ladies of the empire. Who could have believed that the ugly and often unjust word *vanity* could ever be melted down into so true and pretty and flattering a periphrasis!' After many more lengthy extracts he concluded,

> We have withheld our pen from italicising where all is so admirable. We mean exactly what we say, when we assert that the author of *The Angel in the House* has already earned the warm and lasting gratitude of all women, for the profound respect, delicate politeness, and religious chivalry, which are there moulded into a fair poetic form, to the special honour of womanhood.

As was then common practice, the review was anonymous. Emily, at least, knew the author; their friend the poet William Allingham. On the 5th of January she thanked him.[8] 'I have read the remainder of your review in *The Critic* with great pleasure . . .' She promised to show it to Coventry later on, since he had vowed not to read any notices for six months. The only views he would take to heart would be those of his closest friends. The first of these, of course, was Tennyson who by then had become the Poet Laureate. As luck would have it another friend, Aubrey de Vere, also a poet, was able to report from first hand Tennyson's comments on *The Angel* the very moment a copy reached him. De Vere had been on the Isle of Wight, staying at Farringford with the Tennysons. Shortly afterwards he wrote to Coventry.[9]

> I must tell you that never volume of poetry was better treated than your proof sheets. The Tennysons took them & read them sitting on those beautiful downs near the sea: – & neither the charm of the landscape nor the lights on the sea, distracted our attention from the

book. *Alfred said that your poem, when finished, would, as far as he could see, add one more to the small list of "great poems".* After such praise from him all remarks from me must be superfluous yet I must add that it is long since I read anything that seemed to me so beautiful, & to include so much of what is best in nature with what is most felicitous in art, your power of *thinking in verse* & expressing thought in language at once refined & familiar is very remarkable.

Tennyson himself wrote to Coventry,[10] 'Many thanks for your volumes. I still hold that you have written a poem which has a fair chance of immortality; . . . *Little* objections . . . I could make; but, as for the whole, I admire it exceedingly, and trust that it will do our age good, and not ours only. The women ought to subscribe a statue for you.' Praise like this was good to receive. So, too, was a letter from Ruskin. Ruskin wrote on the 2nd November,[11] 'I cannot tell you how much I admire your book. I had no idea you had power of this high kind. I think it will – at all events it ought – to become one of the most pop-ular books in the language – and *blessedly* popular, doing good wherever read.' Coventry thanked him saying, too, how much he had been upset by the critics, even though, keeping his vow, he had only heard about them from Emily. Ruskin counselled him not to worry.[12] 'No thoroughly good thing *can* be praised or felt at once,' he assured him. He had read the poem again and was 'more and more pleased' with it. 'It has purpose & *plain* meaning in every line – it is fit for its age and for all ages, and will gets its place.'

Still, Coventry remained depressed. On two separate occa-sions he wrote to Monckton Milnes,

I sincerely hope that your presages of success may be fulfilled, chiefly because there are five Books yet to come to complete the Poem; and, though I could go on *composing* contentedly enough and confidently enough, *publishing* is a different matter, and I have made up my mind to stop at the *third* failure.[13]

If you see the minor literary journals you will have been somewhat surprised by the contempt with which the 'Angel' has, in most cases, been received . . . Unless one of the great Quarterlies comes to the rescue, my poetical career is at an end; for though while men like yourself, Carlyle, Tennyson, and Ruskin think highly of what I do, my confidence cannot be exhausted, my ability to print books at my own cost and to devote to verse time that could be turned to immediate advantage, is.[14]

For the time being he went on writing, and two years later published *The Espousals*. This was the second volume in the project. In it Felix and Honor wed. The scheme was the same, the criticisms worse. Only his friends kept him going, mostly writers or poets themselves, who understood his literary form and underneath it, what he intended.

Carlyle wrote to him from Annan, on 31st July, 1856.[15]

I had received your beautiful little book, 'Angel of the House, Book II', some time ago, and reserved it for a good opportunity, which I saw ahead. I brought it with me into these parts, the only modern book I took that trouble with; and last night I gave myself the pleasure of a deliberate perusal. Upon which, so favourable was the issue, I now give you the superfluous trouble of my verdict, prior to getting into the Solway for a little swim, the *sound* of which I also hear approaching.

Certainly, it is a beautiful little piece this *Espousals*; nearly perfect in its kind; the execution and conception full of delicacy, truth, and graceful simplicity; high, ingenious, fine, – pure and wholesome as these breezes now blowing round me from the eternal sea. The delineation of the thing is managed with great art, *thrift*, and success, by that light sketching of parts; of which, both in the choice of what is to be delineated, and in the fresh, airy, easy way of doing it, I much admire the genial felicity, the real *skill*. A charming *simplicity* attracts me everywhere; this is a great merit which I am used to in you.

As with Ruskin, Coventry thanked him, yet complaining about the critics. Carlyle told him just to ignore them. Coventry tried but found it impossible. His work simply meant too much to him. Writing to William Bell Scott, another poet and also a painter, who had found his Volume One 'delectable', he told him exactly what he thought of them:[16]

I know something of that basest of trades, Journalism. The man who is not fit, morally or intellectually, for anything honest and regular, becomes a newspaper writer, and the newspaper writer who has not wit or information for any other department of his trade sinks into the poetical critic. I never even see a criticism of my own poetry – for to be excited, as one is apt to be, by praise or blame which one cannot help despising is not wholesome for the mind.

The Angel's sale was not encouraging. Thanks to the con-demnation of the critics, the copies, priced at six shillings, sold only a few per month. Three years had to pass before a cheque arrived from the publisher, and this equalled only his salary for a whole year at the British Museum. He continued to write with stubborn hope. At last the sales began to improve. A long piece by his friend de Vere in the *Edinburgh Review* in 1858 unexpectedly proved a turning point. He learnt too from Aubrey de Vere that the book was 'quite the rage' in America. He gave a copy to Nathaniel Hawthorne, the famous author of *Tanglewood Tales*, who wrote him a warm letter of thanks.[17] The book would be a 'life-long pleasure', one to be prized by himself and his wife as 'one of our fire-side books . . . as long as we live.' His old friend, Thomas Woolner, who often wrote to Mrs Tenny-son, reported on him at this time,[18]

Patmore's own book is selling off well at last; so his turn has come at last; his *Angel* has not met the respect she deserved at the hands of the British Public, and now I suppose the said Public mean to recompense him for old neglect; as you may naturally suppose P. is in good spirits.

I was at J. Parker's on Tuesday evening and there saw Matthew Arnold . . . he made kind enquiries after you who seem to have taken his fancy exceedingly. He was a regular swell, in brilliant white kid gloves, glittering boots and costume cut in most perfect fashion. He had a long talk with Patmore: whose countenance the whole time beamed radiant joy with the satisfaction of holding intercourse with such a high Oxford don of critical propensities.

Still, some of his friends had doubts or, at least, certain anxi-eties; in particular, Richard Garnett, Coventry's British Museum colleague, who kept a critical eye on his work. He was a capable poet himself, and he gave Coventry technical advice as well as comfort and wise warnings about the danger of writing too much. Garnett was very fond of Coventry, and often mentioned him in his letters. In one, to his brother in Manchester, he wrote,[19]

The Angel in the House, to which I alluded in my last, seems to me an elegant and graceful poem, with many remarkable lines and acute remarks. Its subject is a courtship. Patmore's chief defects are a sad lack of invention and imagination. A parody on it which has appeared in the *Athenaeum* was certainly dictated by spite at its having been praised by the *Critic*, and it is a pity that it should condescend to this unworthy mode of warfare.

In another letter, three years later, Garnett returned to the same theme.[20]

What you say about Patmore's egotism is very just – much as I admire *The Angel in the House*, I would not have written it for any money. It is well, then, for literature that all minds are not constituted alike; and it must be owned that if any woman could justify the idolatry of such a poem it would be Mrs Patmore herself.

When Coventry had finished Volume Two, against advice he changed the form and continued in couplets instead of quatrains. Also he carried the story forward by means of letters instead of narrative. Both of these schemes failed, and Volumes Three and Four, *Faithful for Ever* and *Victories of Love*, were each quite simply disastrous. Garnett, asked to review them said,[21]

I never wrote more reluctantly or to less purpose; in fact, when I sent the article it was with the full expectation of having it returned upon my hands ... My dissatisfaction rather concerns the form than the substance of the essay, for I think it a much fairer criticism of the book than has yet appeared ... Patmore has certainly done everything to give his adversaries an appearance of right, and I believe would now admit that my predictions and admonitions while his poem was in progress have been in every respect justified by the result.

One 'result' had been in *The Critic*, once the platform for Allingham's praise, now the mouthpiece for all Coventry's enemies. Reviewing Volume Three it said,[22]

Mr. Coventry Patmore threatens to become an institution. As an accident, we should not have objected to him, and there certainly was just enough sweetness in *The Angel in the House* to make such a composition pass for once in a way; but if we are to have angels in the house every year – cherubs, too, whose waxen rosiness and sweet unmeaning expression make them as like each other as cherries on a stalk – then we feel inclined to cry out . . . The bard of the tea-tables has no place at the banquet of heroes; and if Mr. Patmore publishes any more such compositions as *Faithful for Ever*, he must be satisfied with the lisped plaudits of girls fresh from boarding-schools, still redolent of bread and butter. By others he runs imminent risk of being relegated to that locality which seems to have supplied him with a Christian name.

Naturally, such reviews upset him. Better notices he must have if his great work was ever to survive. Swallowing his pride, he wrote to Monckton Milnes.[23]

I send you a copy of my completed Poem. If you have time to read it again you will find it improved in almost every page. Cannot you get the Editor of the *Times* to give me a column during the Easter recess? I think I have as good a right as *Tannhauser*, Prof. Aytoun, or the 'Lady of La Garaye'. There is fourteen years' conscientious work in the book – which cannot be said of any other Poem since the *Excursion* and its *Prelude*. Moreover the *Times*, unintentionally, did me a great injury. Its onslaught, headed 'Patmore's Friends and Acquaintances' was by the *Public* universally supposed to mean me; for my father had written nothing for a quarter of a century, and I was the only 'Patmore' known to them by name.

This was in 1862. Something else took place this year to add to Coventry's state of misery. It was far worse than literary failure, and affected his whole life and family. Emily, his wife, his 'Angel', was dying. For some time she had suffered from consumption; now her condition was clearly hopeless. She had only a matter of months to live, and there was nothing else to be done except to prepare for the end with composure. She had taken all the necessary steps, written her will and chosen her grave. It was in the country, as she wished: in the burial ground, on a little hill, of St Mary's Church at Hendon.

CHAPTER EIGHT

Emily's Death. The Start of the Legend

A T THE TIME of Emily Patmore's death the disease of the lungs known as 'phthisis' (from the Greek meaning 'to waste away') – in England popularly known as 'consumption' (derived from the Latin verb *consumo* meaning, ominously 'I destroy') – was found everywhere, could not be cured, and was understood by the medical profession only as being a type of tuberculosis.

The symptoms, of course, were well known: the constant coughing; the spitting of blood; the hectic flush; the brilliant eye; privately, within the family, the diarrhoea, vomiting and sweating; for women, also, period cessation. All these were seen by everyone as being signals of the greatest danger. Cure, however, was another matter. Plenty of rest and good food, fresh air and appropriate exercise – all were known to delay the advance, sometimes for quite a number of years. Then the symptoms would show again. Whatever the doctor might advise and however the patient might submit, in the end there was no escape. Once the illness was diagnosed, Death was outside the bedroom door and the sufferer could only whisper 'Open, Sesame'.

In Emily's case, the first symptoms came as a result of a bad cold, caught while nursing her latest child, a little girl called Bertha. She knew the fatal signals well, not only because they were common knowledge (of all the deaths in England and Wales, one in six was from consumption), but also because she had nursed her mother in the far distant days at Walworth when she, too, had sickened and died of it. She went to the seaside to rest immediately, and after a while appeared to recover. Still, she had to be very careful. Coventry wrote to Dante Rossetti,[1] 'My wife has been dangerously ill and though danger is now, I trust, over, she is so weak that she will have to keep her room and bed probably for several weeks yet.' For a while the cure appeared to be complete. Then the danger appeared again. Once more she fled to the seaside. This time she was very ill. Although again she seemed to recover she knew that sooner or later she was bound to succumb. She wrote a farewell letter to Coventry which he found by chance, before she died, during a last, illusory respite.[2]

> I leave my wedding-ring to your second wife with my love and blessing ... also, I leave you my grateful acknowledgement of your goodness and love to me, my last prayer that God may bless and console you, my first, last, and only love. If in a year or two you are able to marry again, do so happily, feeling that if my spirit can watch you, it will love her who makes you happy, and not envy her the reward of a part of your love, the best years of which I have had.

In spite of illness, she had more children, another girl and another boy. He was christened Henry John, the second name in honour of Ruskin whom she had asked to be his god-father. Eventually she became too weak to look after herself. Her younger sister Georgiana, who had married Coventry's brother George, and was, unhappily, already widowed (he had died of fever near Mozambique) moved up from Avenue Road to stay in the house and look after her.

During the weeks of inactivity Emily wrote *The Servant's Behaviour Book*; verses and stories to amuse children – *Nursery Poetry* and *Nursery Tales*; and, for parents as well as the young, a collection of poems called *The Children's Garland*, which she and Coventry compiled together, with a frontispiece by Woolner. She wrote also reviews and articles, principally in the *Derby Mercury*, of which Coventry's brother, Gurney, happened to be the literary editor. In the intervals, she wrote letters. Half in fun and half in earnest her nephew Forester Andrews in Australia, aged then fourteen, the son of her eldest brother Edward, had asked her consent to marry Honour, her third child and eldest daughter. Her reply was sensible and also loving.[3]

MY DEAR FORESTER

Since you propose to become my son-in-law as well as my nephew I am anxious to know more about you. Will you write and tell me if you are good tempered and industrious, whether you intend to persevere in whatever profession or business your father choose for you and whether your constancy may be depended on for 15 years for I cannot let Honor marry till she is 18.

She is on a visit to an old nurse at Gravesend just now. I went yesterday to see her and she was looking pretty enough to win a thousand hearts. Her little laughter is like a silver bell, and she sings like a little bird. I told her that her cousin Forester wished her to become his wife, and to go and live with him in another country till he was rich enough to bring her back – that he would be very kind to her and give her a kangaroo, then I said 'What shall I tell him?' Therewith she clasped her little hands together, and looking serious replied 'Tell him I will doe and be hid little wife'. So now you know her mind. As for me, I will agree that if when you are 15 years older you come to England with enough money to remain, and still wish to have her, you may try to make her like you enough to say then 'I will be his little wife'. This is however supposing that you are good and gentlemanly, as I have no doubt you will be. Perhaps, however, you will like Bertha better, I will tell you about her when she is older. I cannot send you any of Honor's hair, because it has never been cut, but I enclose a small piece of Tennyson's, which is the same colour, so that you can, for the present fancy it Honor's.

Your affectionate aunt.
E. A. PATMORE

Other letters at this time were addressed to those who were closer to home. Especially she wrote to her son Tennyson, then aged twelve years, away at school at Christ's Hospital, where he had found a place thanks to a nomination from Ruskin. That she was very ill she well knew, and did not conceal the fact in her letters.[4]

I am a little better than I was when you were here [she wrote in one]. Honor & Bertha send their love. I have let them have the top once, but I intend only to give it out very seldom. Mrs Gemmer says your letter was a very nice little one, and pleased her very much.

Good bye and good night, my dear boy, and may God bless you and give you grace to keep all your good resolutions.

Your fond MAMA

[In another she wrote,[5]] The doctor has been to see me today and we had to pay a guinea. He says I may easily be ill again, and must do almost nothing, and I must have no worry of any kind.

The Child's Garland is published now, and is a very pretty book. You shall see it when you come home.

> Good bye dear. I am your fond MAMA

She sent him the last on 2nd June, 1862, only a few weeks before her death.[6]

I am about the same as when you saw me. I shall soon have you singing by me again, for the leave day is in a week.

Monday was Emily's birthday. Aunt Georgie and little Eliza came and we had tea on the lawn. I was there, too. Papa made me a sort of bed to lie on.

Mrs Jackson and her daughter are going on Saturday to stay with your godfather & godmother. I dare say they will tell him what a nice good tempered little fellow you are.

> Good bye Pet,
> MAMA

Coventry wrote to Tennyson, too; not sparing him any anxiety,[7]

I write to remind you of your promise to work hard and regain your place at the upper part of your class. You must know that you have been disappointing us a good deal lately, and that it has not been without many a heartache that I and your Mama have seen your chance of being a Grecian growing less and less. We feel sure that, if you chose, you might get one of the cleverer boys at the head of your class to tell you what your Ovid means when you cannot find out.

Remember, my dear little boy, that you are not likely to have your poor Mama long. Although she does not look very ill, she is really much worse than she was a year ago, and she is *sure* not to live very long. So you should make the best of the time you have left to please her. It will be very unhappy, when she is gone, to think that you might have made her happier and did not do so.

But, although your learning is very important, there are other things much more important. To be always strictly honest, always to tell the simple truth, and to be *pure* (you know what I mean) are the *most* important things. When the other boys say and do dirty things (as many boys at all great schools will) remember those words of Jesus Christ 'The pure in heart shall see God' – that is to say, they will go to heeaven. If you are not pure, you will not only not see God, but you will not see your dear Mama any more when she is gone.

Cannot you get Mr. Simon's nephew (who is now Deputy Grecian) to help you with your Ovid? You may ask him to come and spend the afternoon with us if you like, your next holiday; and you can dine in Percy Street, and go afterwards to Elm Cottage and take Wolf out a walk.

Your affectionate Father

C. PATMORE

The last letter that Emily wrote was addressed to a friend, Caroline Gemmer, otherwise known as Gerda Fay, a poetess of some ability.[8] She knew the end was very near; she had, in fact, a month to live.

June 4th 1862

DEAR MRS GEMMER,

There are few days that I can write, and I have my two boys & others very near to me who claim all I can give of my strength, but as I fondly believe – and indeed my hitherto hopeful physician has told me I cannot recover – though possibly I may rally a little – I must send you a 'God bless you' in my own hand.

I lie loosely dressed outside the bed from which I never move except on fine days when I am carried by Mr. Patmore to a bed in a carriage for a drive, or to be in the garden, under a shady tree.

I have a governess for the children, excellent nursing, besides my dear husband and luxuries of every kind sent by friends and even strangers, lovers of my husband's poetry. Every earthly comfort, and the most excellent gift of happy temper & good spirits.

Death is a delightful prospect to me except when my faith grows weak about those I am to leave: so do not pity, but rather envy me.

I would not change my place with any living creature. I have not a shadow of natural animal fear of death. Truly I may say 'Oh death where is thy sting, O grave, where is thy victory'.

I feel you love me enough to like to hear this. I seldom write of religion, I so dread unintentional exaggeration.

Now God bless you and all dear to you. I do not think I shall send you another letter.

Yours affectionately

EMILY A. PATMORE

Honor shall write if there is any decided change good or bad. I have been for weeks much like this but always slowly getting thinner and weaker.

[Written inside the flap of the envelope:] It was only a few hours after my last short letter to you that the haemorrhage came on which laid me up again.

One last joy had been given her. In March her eldest son Milnes had passed his exam to enter the Naval college at Dartmouth. Coventry had written to Monckton Milnes in November, 1861.[9] 'Pray accept my most hearty thanks for your kindness in having used your influence so effectually in favor of my boy. I only hope that he will be persuaded to take as much trouble to secure his own advantage as you have taken in obtaining for him the opportunity.' In March he wrote again:[10] 'I have just got a telegraphic despatch to say that Milly has passed. The examination was over last Friday, but the result was not made known till today. When shall I bring him to say good-bye to you in his uniform?' Two weeks later, another report came through to Milnes.[11] 'My boy seems to be doing his very best to set himself right with Admiral Eden. Looking out of port-holes during school-hours and lying in bed two minutes after the drum beats are sins which he confesses to, and is heartily abjuring.' The optimistic note continued in April.[12] 'We have had several letters from the Cadet, each written in higher glee than the last, and all evidently indicating that his new mode of life will suit him exactly. The relief and comfort are inexpressible of having been able to see him set going in a career which will at once utilize and discipline the energies that would probably have made him, and everyone about him, uncomfortable, in any other way of life.'

So at least Emily's fears, the natural worries of a loving mother for the education and future prospects of both her sons, Milnes and Tennyson, were that year assuaged. The fatal haemorrhage that brought the end started only a short interval after her farewell letter to Mrs Gemmer. Her eldest daughter, Honor, described it.[13]

We, as I said, went to Hampstead in the summer. She grew worse, and after my ninth birthday, 2nd of June, she was very ill. One evening I had said good-night and came back to fetch a book. She was sitting in that folding cane arm-chair which is in the entrance, with one hand on its arm, and her head leaned back, as if very weak . . . Soon after, I heard all the bells in the house ringing, everyone running about, Papa calling my brothers, and Mama calling for 'the children'. I was very much frightened, but stayed in bed. The next day we heard she was very ill; we went to Mrs Jackson's for a week (Bertha and I); when we came back, the funeral was over. Papa came for us in a cab. I asked how she was, and he said, 'Better than she has ever been' (I was so glad for a moment), but he added 'for she is in heaven.' . . . She was insensible for three days, and died on Saturday at midnight, like our Lord being three days in the grave and rising at that time . . . Just before her death, we used to feed the sparrows a great deal, and at last they used to eat off her very pillows. . . . I remember her making shirts for Papa in the bed in which she died.

Coventry himself wrote about her death in a poem he called 'Departure'.[14]

It was not like your great and gracious ways!
Do you, that have nought other to lament,
Never, my Love, repent
Of how, that July afternoon,
You went,
With sudden, unintelligible phrase,
And frighten'd eye,
Upon your journey of so many days,
Without a single kiss or a good-bye?
I knew, indeed, that you were parting soon;
And so we sate, within the low sun's rays,
You whispering to me, for your voice was weak,
Your harrowing praise.
Well, it was well
To hear you such things speak,
And I could tell
What made your eyes a growing gloom of love,
As a warm South-wind sombres a March grove.
And it was like your great and gracious ways
To turn your talk on daily things, my Dear,
Lifting the luminous, pathetic lash,
To let the laughter flash,
Whilst I drew near,

Because you spoke so low that I could scarcely hear.
But all at once to leave me at the last
More at the wonder than the loss aghast,
With huddled, unintelligible phrase,
And frightened eye,
And go your journey of all days
With not one kiss or a good-bye,
And the only loveless look the look with which you pass'd,
'Twas all unlike your great and gracious ways.

Close to the end she spoke of Woolner – Thomas Woolner, whom she had always loved. What she said is not recorded. Also she talked of Dr Andrews, and how he had hated the Roman Catholics. Coventry, she knew, was leaning towards them. With premonition she said, 'When I am gone, they will get you; and then I shall see you no more.'[15] In her last hours she suffered convulsions.[16] When they stopped, she slipped away – 'With huddled, unintelligible phrase,' – as though, somehow, she wished to speak but found 'Farewell' a word too difficult to say.

CHAPTER NINE

Coventry's Death. The Angel Triumphs

T HE YEAR following Emily's death brought another family disaster from which, at least, she was shielded by the hand of Providence. The beloved Milly, the eldest son, who had proudly entered the Naval College, thanks to his godfather's intercession, was sacked for idleness and misbehaviour. Coventry had written to him quite explicitly, having received an official warning, on 6th March, 1863.[1]

MY DEAR BOY,

I am overwhelmed with sorrow and surprise at receiving a letter from Mr. Milnes, inclosing another letter from Admiral Eden, who tells Mr. Milnes that '*If the boy does not improve he had better be taken away*' and saying that your character is unsatisfactory '*in study, in seamanship and especially in conduct*'.

I tell you plainly that, under these circumstances, if I do have to take you away, I shall place you '*before the mast*' in a merchant ship; for I see that, after all, your purposes and promises of amendment cannot be trusted, and that nothing but the discipline you will get as a common sea-boy will probably bring you to your senses.

I shall send you your new uniform down next week, as you may as well have the use of it during the short time you are likely to be allowed the unmerited honour of remaining in Her Majesty's Navy.

I advise you to postpone your Confirmation until some future time. You cannot be in a proper state to take your Christian vows upon yourself, when you have so far forgotten the vows, made beside your Mother's coffin, as to bring down on you the disgrace of this letter from Admiral Eden.

Your Affectionate Father,
COVENTRY PATMORE

Milly could not repent, no doubt too upset by his mother's death and his father's dictatorial attitude. Events had to take their course. So he was banished 'before the mast', one of the hardest lives in existence, and put on a ship that was bound for India. By the next Christmas he was far away among, as his father jocosely put it, 'his swearing, grog-drinking shipmates'.

Coventry's misery at this time emerges plainly in all his letters, sometimes overflowing in wrath, as it did in his letters to Milly; sometimes in tender sentimentality as it did to his other son, away at school at Christ's Hospital. 'My dear Tenny,' he wrote, a year after Emily's death,[2]

Your account of your place in the class of Great Erasmus is very satisfactory. If you knew how much more I love you than I did before you began to work so heartily you would be very happy.

I send you 18 stamps; 6 for letters and 12 for pocket-money. Your loving Father, C. Patmore.

Remember, Dear, that tomorrow at 6 o'clock was the time your dear Mama began to die, and that her agony lasted till midnight on the fifth, that is next Sunday. In this, as in all things, she was like Christ, who, you know, was three days in hell before he went into his glory. So your heavenly Mother was three days in her death-agony before the angels carried her to everlasting bliss, where she waits for you and me.

Coventry's state of grief and depression even led him to break with the Ormes. They were the best friends he ever had and his sister-in-law Georgiana had nursed Emily up to the last. In a long letter written to Brett he related,[3]

We see nothing now of the Ormes. I waited six months during which time Mrs Orme and Georgiana called *once* on the four little orphans. So, when at Xmas Mrs Orme made one of her children write to Tennyson to say she (the child) hoped to see him during the holidays, I wrote to Mr. Orme to say that unless the ladies of his house chose to pay me & the children a little more attention than that, I should prefer a complete cessation of intercourse. Which last alternative they have – to my relief – chosen.

By the autumn of 1863, fifteen months after Emily's death, Coventry's health began to fail. At his best he had never been strong, and he now developed a dangerous cough. It was obvious to all that he must go away and try to recover his strength and spirits, or he would soon be really ill and maybe, like Emily, die of consumption. So he obtained a doctor's certificate, and was given leave by the Trustees to take a rest for four months. Boarding the children with friends in Hampstead, in February, 1864, he left London to spend the spring in Italy.

This visit in two ways entirely changed the course of his life. In Rome he met Aubrey de Vere, his old friend and fellow-poet who, being a Roman Catholic, introduced him to Catholic Society. Just exactly as Emily had warned, he was soon persuaded to change his faith, his natural inclination to mysticism finding in Roman Catholic practice the means it sought for expression. Thus if Emily's view was correct – her fear conveyed before she died – he condemned them both to eternal divorce; to live for ever in different spheres in the next world as well as the present; to see each other no more. At the same time he became engaged to a Roman Catholic called Marianne Byles, herself a convert to Roman Catholicism. She had been received into the church by Cardinal Manning, who later on in the summer married them. Very shy and so reserved that hardly anyone got to know her or left a record of what she was like, she cared for Coventry's children well, and proved a loving, if silent partner. Coventry described her to Edward Andrews, his brother-in-law in South Australia,[4]

I met the lady in Rome, and was first attracted by a great likeness to Emily, both in person and manners – a likeness which has grown upon me ever since. I need not say more than this to assure you of my and the children's advantage. She is the same age as Emily would have been had she lived; and has a *very* large fortune – a fact of which I was in complete ignorance until several days after our engagement.

Thanks to her wealth, which became his own under the existing laws of marriage, he achieved financial freedom at last. So he resigned from the British Museum. Like his father Peter George, long before at Mill Hill in the happy days of sufficient money, he decided to move to the country. He bought a fine estate in Sussex, enlarged the house, improved the grounds, and adopted the role of a landed gentleman. Also, of course, he continued to write. He began to experiment with complex rhythms and lines of greater and shorter length in which he composed a series of odes of a sensual, religious and mystical character. These were privately printed but then destroyed because of a poor response from his friends. He wrote, too, a descriptive poem which found its way into all the anthologies. It was called 'The Toys', and inspired by a drama which had taken place long before between himself and a youthful Milly.[5]

> My little Son, who look'd from thoughtful eyes,
> And moved and spoke in quiet grown-up wise,
> Having my law the seventh time disobey'd,
> I struck him, and dismiss'd
> With hard words and unkiss'd,
> His Mother, who was patient, being dead.
> Then, fearing lest his grief should hinder sleep,
> I visited his bed,
> But found him slumbering deep,
> With darken'd eyelids, and their lashes yet
> From his late sobbing wet.
> And I, with moan,
> Kissing away his tears, left others of my own;
> For, on a table drawn beside his head,
> He had put, within his reach,
> A box of counters and a red-vein'd stone,
> A piece of glass abraded by the beach,
> And six or seven shells,
> A bottle with bluebells,
> And two French copper coins, ranged there with careful art,
> To comfort his sad heart.
> So, when that night I pray'd
> To God, I wept, and said;
> Ah, when at last we lie with tranced breath,
> Not vexing Thee in death,
> And Thou rememberest of what toys
> We made our joys,
> How weakly understood,
> Thy great commanded good,
> Then, fatherly not less
> Than I whom Thou has moulded from the clay,
> Thou'lt leave Thy wrath, and say,
> 'I will be sorry for their childishness.'

In fact, at the time of composition, Milly was far away at sea, long past the days of childhood, still suffering Coventry's wrath for having failed to survive at Dartmouth. For the son, already deeply hurt, 'The Toys' must really have been the last straw, compounding a dictatorial act with hypocritical sentimentality.★ The public, however, acclaimed the poem and saw it only as confirmation of their own view of Coventry's nature. The shy author of *The Angel in the House* was not only a perfect spouse but also a stern as well as loving, pious paterfamilias.

His reputation as a moral guide, lighting the home with a beacon of love, was also increased by Ruskin. He had always admired *The Angel*, and when he published *Of Queens' Gardens* (the second part of *Sesame and Lilies*) in the course of 1865, his treatise on perfect womanly behaviour, he praised *The Angel* and its author.[6] 'You cannot read him too often or too carefully;' he wrote, 'as far as I know he is the only living poet who always strengthens and purifies . . . Know you not those lovely lines – I would they were learned by all youthful ladies of England:–

> Ah, wasteful woman, she who may
> On her sweet self set her own price,
> Knowing he cannot choose but pay,
> How she has cheapen'd Paradise;'

Ruskin quoted *The Angel*, too, in 'Wheat-Sifting', the tenth letter in *Time and Tide*, 'Twenty-five letters to a working man of Sunderland'.[7] 'Take, for instance, that which, in its purity, is the source of the highest and purest mortal happiness – Love . . . – as you have it expressed, for instance, thus, exquisitely, in the *Angel in the House*:– '

> And there, with many blissful tear,
> I vowed to love and prayed to wed
> The maiden who had grown so dear; –
> Thanked God, who had set her in my path;

★ Students of Joseph Conrad's work believe that in *Chance* Conrad took Coventry as his model for 'the late Carleon Anthony, the "poet tyrant" '. If this is correct, and if, as is thought, Conrad obtained his information from Milly, the latter achieved a lasting revenge. See *Review of English Studies, 20, (1969)* page 468, in which this attribution is examined in detail.

Ruskin was still a leading critic, and anything he wrote was widely read. *Sesame and Lilies* had a huge sale and, as a result, Coventry's work came to the notice of a new class and a whole new literary audience which adopted, too, his popular image as Love's domestic spokesman. An 'Angel' cult had already begun, indeed, at the very highest level. The Prince of Wales had recently married the daughter of Christian IX of Denmark. 'We triumph in their vision of wedded love,' one journalist had written of Edward and Alexandra, 'We rejoice that "the Angel in the House" has come to dwell in the Royal Palace.'[8] The book, too, was selling steadily, especially to newly married couples. It was 'a good wedding gift to a bridegroom from his friends', as one masculine enthusiast put it.[9]

Still, Coventry remained depressed. '*I* am become utterly idle through utter hopelessness,' he wrote to his old friend, Mrs Gemmer, in August, 1870.[10] Three years later he asked Macmillan, who had published a fourth edition of *The Angel*, to sell him all the remaining copies. This was agreed for £50. Once safely back in his hands, Coventry built a huge bonfire and ceremoniously burnt the lot as though he hoped to burn his sorrow with them. In the following years, as taste changed and as new schools of poetry emerged, *The Angel* appeared to contemporary readers to be out of date and rather ridiculous. It was only remembered because of its title which came into use more and more to symbolise perfect, wifely behaviour. 'Most (husbands) are warmly grateful, and recognise the value of the angel in the house, who is not too angelic to know what goes on in the kitchen, down to the very drains', wrote the well-known authoress, Mrs Haweis in her *Art of Housekeeping, A Bridal Garland.*[11]

Cartoonists took up the phrase, too, as a useful tag for some of their jokes. One in *Punch* drew Lydia Becker, a prominent worker for Women's Rights, making a speech in the House of Commons.[12] Beside her lay a ball of wool; she was knitting, of course, a 'blue stocking'. The caption read: 'The Angel in "The House", the result of Female Suffrage (A Troubled Dream of the Future).' Swinburne, a poet greater than Coventry, lowered himself to write a parody in his pamphlet, 'Specimens of Modern Poets'.[13] He called it 'The Person of the House', and in it described in Coventry's metre the happy birth of a first child, the husband entering the nuptial bedroom

> My spirit, in the doorway's pause,
>   Fluttered with fancies in my breast;
> Obsequious to all decent laws,
>   I felt exceedingly distressed.

Domestic tragedy struck Coventry again, as he reached the end of his fifth decade. His eldest daughter Honor, who had become a nun, died and so did his youngest son, Henry, an aspiring poet. Worst of all, his wife died after a marriage of fifteen years, a union as long as his and Emily's. A year later he married again to Harriet Robson, the children's governess, a step that was not approved by the family although she made him, in his own words, 'a thoroughly good and sweet little wife'. He should have been happy, but he was not. Except for 'The Toys' and similar pieces of short, simple, narrative character, he had written only *The Unknown Eros*, a work of quasi-sensual Catholicism which neither his friends nor the public had liked. His life as a poet seemed to be over. He sold his estate and moved to Hastings to an old house he had always admired. From there he wrote to Mrs Gemmer, in February, 1882, 'It seems to me that you ought to think yourself very lucky if you find life only "something like a term of mild penal servitude". *My* poetic glimpses of the possible have not left me so great a resignation to the actual.'[14] In this mood he spent his time, writing only critical prose; reading and taking long walks; leading the life of an elderly recluse; lost in a fog of doubt and literary misery.

In the spring of 1887, something happened which cheered him up. The respected publishing house of Cassell decided to market cheap editions of many of literature's greatest works, from Plutarch down to Charles Dickens, selecting more than two hundred titles.

Designed to appeal to a new readership, the poorer, simpler, literate classes, their price of threepence, or 'in cloth, sixpence', only the cost of a jug of beer, and a tenth of the price of usual productions, proved an unexpected attraction. Lord Macaulay's essay on *Warren Hastings* was given the place of number one;

Dickens' *Chimes* was fifty-two; Plutarch's *Lives* was fifty-eight; and, to Coventry's great delight, his *Angel* appeared as number seventy. The editor, Professor Henry Morley, wrote in the Introduction:

There could be but one answer to the suggestion of Mr. Coventry Patmore that his *Angel in the House* might usefully have a place in this 'National Library' . . . the best use of writing is fulfilled by the spreading of verses dedicated to sacred love of home. The two parts of the Poem appeared in 1854 and 1856 . . . and have since obtained a permanent place among the Home Books of the English People. Our readers will join, surely, in thanks to the author for the present he has made us.

The professor's hopes were fully realised. The success of *The Angel* was quite spectacular. Returns from bookshops throughout the country reported a sale in the first fortnight of more than 40,000 copies. The reason for this was largely historical. It was now more than thirty years since the publication of the first edition, and a generation not born when *The Angel* first appeared in print found its picture of Sarum Close and the Dean's simple daughter, Honor, who visited the poor, feared to waltz, and fell in love by Stonehenge, as out of date as the coach and the crinoline, and just as quaint, romantic and charming.

The year was that of the Jubilee, and all thoughts were turned to the past when Queen Victoria had come to the throne; to the days of simple English life before the close of the Coaching Era; before too many factories had scarred the land and the cities choked the air with smoke. Thus *The Angel*'s plot and background exactly caught the mood of the times. Its sales continued to spiral up. Before the end of Coventry's life, at least according to several estimates, they had nearly topped the million.

Naturally, Coventry's spirits revived. 'My Dear Mrs Jackson,'* he wrote to his and Emily's old friend,[15]

---

* Mrs Jackson's daughter, Julia, was the mother of Virginia Woolf, and thus the friendship between Coventry and the Jackson family must have made the history of Emily's death and *The Angel in the House* a familiar topic of conversation when Virginia was a child. In view of Virginia's subsequent determination to 'kill' the Angel (see Introduction) this connection is interesting.

It was very friendly of you to remember my birthday. It is curious that, at 64, I find myself in every way better in health than I have ever been before, and almost as strong in muscle. We have made the terrace into an archery-ground, and I find I can shoot with the strongest bow at a target 80 yards off just as well as I could at Heron's Ghyll 20 years ago. And, on the whole, I find myself happier than I have ever been. Piffie* is a continual delight, beyond all I ever dreamt of; and if I have few other keener pleasures, I have much more peace of mind.

He wrote also to Thomas Woolner, the only one of the Pre-Raphaelites with whom he had kept in close contact. Coventry's letter has not survived, but Woolner's was carefully kept by the family.[16] 'The Angel's success is simply wonderful, and surely among so vast a number some must be able to appreciate and be all the better for it. I should like to hear that the Angel had multiplied to the extent of 300,000 and more if readers could be found. I should think it is the cheapest 3d worth ever issued!' Woolner wrote again a few months later:[17] 'I was glad and amazed to know that the cheap edition had made the other sell more; this is very good, and as it should be. If we were not going down almost as fast as a nation can go I should say that things may begin to mend soon; but during the most degraded career some little redeeming traits of virtue sometimes show themselves.'

Many strangers wrote to him too. J. H. Goring of 222 New North Road, London, did so in a poem of sixty-two lines.[18]

> O pure and lofty Bard! thy song
> So sweet and true has made me long
> For Heaven, where my spirit may
> Meet thine, and in some sort repay
> My hopelessly deep debt to thee
> For thy seraphic melody.
>
> I read thy pages o'er and o'er
> And know thee better, love thee more.

* Piffie was Coventry's son by his third wife, Harriet, born four years previously in January, 1883, whose full name was Francis Joseph Mary Epiphanius.

I share thy hopes, thy creed believe,
For as I read, Sir, I perceive
Thou art a prophet, making clear
The ways of God. If this appear
To some, profanity of praise –
For men, alas! refuse to gaze
On Truth near by, but strain their eyes
To distant days and other skies
I can but speak of things I know,
And all my soul affirms it so.
And why not?

Receiving tributes such as these, even Coventry could not doubt the real success of his poem for Emily. *The Angel* was, as *The Times* said, 'an uncontested English Classic'.[19] Referring back to Oliver Goldsmith and his famous play, *She Stoops to Conquer*, published as Cassell's Number 12 in the same series as *The Angel*, *The Illustrated London News* gave it an even greater tribute. From the empyrean heights of poetry *the Angel in the House* had come down to earth. Read in more than a million homes, it had 'stooped to conquer the multitude'.[20]

Coventry's joy was not prolonged. Thanks to an ill-advised remark by the poet Gerard Manley Hopkins who had thought *The Angel* a 'basket of violets' but had not liked *Sponsa Dei*, his latest collection of mystical odes, he once again became depressed. He burnt the odes and reverted to prose. He had also sent a copy to Tennyson who had only thanked him with one line. He had not seen him for many years having, after Emily's death, felt that Tennyson had wished to drop him. This was certainly incorrect, and only due to a lost letter, but Tennyson's curt thanks for his odes seemed to confirm his earlier impression and deepened further his mood of dejection. Once again he wrote to Woolner,[21] '. . . as I get older I value more the very few friends whom death or the vitiating effects of fame have left me . . . Every day I live makes this rotten hole, the world, more hateful to me. Only let us try that it may be Purgatory, not Hell to us.'

'I have been very poorly ever since the great frost ceased,' he wrote the following spring to his future biographer, Basil

Champneys.[22] 'While it lasted, I was in the highest health. Since then, the most likely feeling I can get up, is one which enables me to say with Clough, "I can wait to die". But as I am half-way through my sixty-eighth year I suppose this is as much as I can reasonably expect.' He had, in fact, five years ahead of him; *The Angel* had made him a literary lion, and wherever he went in these years, in the fashionable world or artistic society, he was met with awe and heard with reverence. His portrait was painted by John Sargent, the foremost society artist of the day, and, on the death of Alfred Tennyson, his name was canvassed for Poet Laureate. He was not appointed, so it was joked, because the Premier, William Gladstone, had thought the proposal only a tease, as everyone knew that Coventry, too, was dead.

His own choice had been Alice Meynell with whom he had formed an intimate friendship. As a woman, she had no chance, the post being always held by a man; but, by merely proposing her name, Coventry had wished to promote her poetry. He had found in her an understanding of all his work, after *The Angel*, which the general public had always denied him. For several years he saw her continually, using her London house as his own, sending her private poems for criticism, writing her long and intense letters, giving her some of his greatest treasures, including a manuscript of *The Angel*. To his great distress, she stopped seeing him, quite suddenly, for a private reason. It was said to be at her husband's urgent wish, because Coventry had tried to kiss her. She was thirty years younger than he was, the same age as his wife, Harriet, who had found the connection extremely tiresome. Perhaps, as it was commonly supposed, poetic interest had turned to love. Alice had seen this and drawn away to avoid the inevitable, painful, disastrous consequences.

Another sorrow at this time was having to leave his home at Hastings, a house he had known and loved since childhood, his landlord refusing to renew his lease. He moved to a villa in Lymington in Hampshire. Then, too, there was Woolner's funeral, an occasion of extra special sorrow, not only because of their lifelong friendship but also because, by an odd chance, he was buried at Hendon, next to Emily. Emily's grave had become unkempt, and Coventry ordered its restoration and the re-leading of its plain lettering:*

EMILY WIFE OF COVENTRY PATMORE

From this time onwards, his health declined. On a visit to London he wrote to Harriet, complaining of fits of dizziness and faintness. He was found to be suffering from angina pectoris. A few months afterwards, his heart failed him. On a cold, damp November day he took a walk to a local hotel to read the paper and smoke a cigarette, an hotel that happened to be called 'The Angel'. On his way back he caught a chill. Three days later he passed away. Born in 1823 and dying in 1896, he was therefore aged seventy-three. Only the family attended the funeral. Robed as a Franciscan friar, of which Order he had been a tertiary, he was laid to rest, as he desired, in a Roman Catholic cemetery.

While Emily's death had been unrecorded except in Coventry's subsequent verse, his, of course, received attention. The great arbiters of public taste like *The Spectator* and *The Athenaeum* which earlier had mocked his work so cruelly took occasion to make amends. *The Spectator* said that he ought to have been made the Poet Laureate instead of Alfred Austin.[23] *The Athenaeum* wrote, 'Patmore's domestic muse, whom he loved and celebrated with all his skill, was his wife, that veritable 'Angel in the House' to whom he devoted a collection of exquisite psalms of love such as husband never wrote before ...'[24] *The Times* gave him more than a whole column. *Punch* even made up a little verse which ended,[25]

> The raptures of the spirit spouse
> To him were no elusive dream
> Who wrote *The Angel in the House*!

Similar praise came from every quarter.

After thirty-four years, if not in Heaven, at least on Earth, *The Angel*'s author, Coventry Patmore and his first wife, Emily

---

* Emily's grave is officially indexed as being No. 89 in Area 2. The descriptive stone, shown upright in the photograph facing page 158 of Vol. I. of Champney's biography is now flat, the balustrading, etc. having been vandalised. Woolner's tomb also has been neglected.

Andrews, were re-united in the obituaries. They were the couple the public knew – together they shared its final blessing. They were the poem's hero and heroine, the ward and daughter of the Dean of Salisbury. It did not matter that this was wrong; that neither had ever lived or stayed there. So far as the world was concerned, they had. There they had met and fallen in love, she had given her hand in marriage and had proved his inspiration. There, in tranquil Sarum Close, she had won her literary immortality. There she was Emily, the wife of Coventry; the honoured spouse of the famous poet; the personification of wifely duty; his Angel in the House.

The Angel in the House

*The text of the last separately printed edition,
published by Harrap in 1923 as one of their Sesame Booklets,
and containing the final versions of Books I and II.*

Book I

THE PROLOGUE

'Mine is no horse with wings, to gain
  The region of the spheral chime;
He does but drag a rumbling wain,
  Cheer'd by the silver bells of rhyme;
And if at Fame's bewitching note
  My homely Pegasus pricks an ear,
The world's cart-collar hugs his throat,
  And he's too wise to kick or rear.'

Thus ever answer'd Vaughan his wife,
  Who, more than he, desired his fame;
But, in his heart, his thoughts were rife
  How for her sake to earn a name.
With bays poetic three times crown'd,
  And other college honours won,
He, if he chose, might be renown'd,
  He had but little doubt, she none;
And in a loftier phrase he talk'd
  With her, upon their Wedding-Day,
(The eighth), while through the fields they
    walk'd,
  Their children shouting by the way.

'Not careless of the gift of song,
  Nor out of love with noble fame,
I, meditating much and long
  What I should sing, how win a name,
Considering well what theme unsung,
  What reason worth the cost of rhyme,
Remains to loose the poet's tongue
  In these last days, the dregs of time,

Learn that to me, though born so late,
  There does, beyond desert, befall
(May my great fortune make me great!)
  The first of themes sung last of all.
In green and undiscover'd ground,
  Yet near where many others sing,
I have the very well-head found
  Whence gushes the Pierian Spring.'

Then she: 'What is it, Dear? The Life
  Of Arthur, or Jerusalem's Fall?'
'Neither: your gentle self, my wife,
  And love, that grows from one to all.
And if I faithfully proclaim
  Of these the exceeding worthiness,
Surely the sweetest wreath of Fame
  Shall, to your hope, my brows caress;
And if, by virtue of my choice
  Of this, the most heart-touching theme
That ever tuned a poet's voice,
  I live, as I am bold to dream,
To be delight to future days,
  And into silence only cease
When those are still, who shared their bays
  With Laura and with Beatrice.
Imagine, Dear, how learned men
  Will deep-conceived devices find,
Beyond my purpose and my ken,
  An ancient bard of simple mind!
You, Sweet, his Mistress, Wife, and Muse,
  Were you for mortal woman meant?
Your praises give a hundred clues
  To mythological intent!
And, severing thus the truth from trope,
  In you the Commentators see,

Some Faith, some Charity, some Hope,
  Some, wiser, think you all the three.'
She laugh'd. How proud she always was
  To see how proud he was of her!
But he had grown distraught, because
  The Muse's mood began to stir.

The Cathedral Close

PRELUDE

Love's Reality

I walk, I trust, with open eyes;
  I've travell'd half my worldly course;
And in the way behind me lies
  Much vanity and some remorse;
I've lived to feel how pride may part
  Spirits, tho' match'd like hand and glove;
I've blush'd for love's abode, the heart;
  But have not disbelieved in love;
Nor unto love, sole mortal thing
  Of worth immortal, done the wrong
To count it, with the rest that sing,
  Unworthy of a serious song;
And love is my reward; for now,
  When most of dead'ning time complain,
The myrtle blooms upon my brow,
  Its odour quickens all my brain.

Love's Immortality

How vilely 'twere to misdeserve
  The poet's gift of perfect speech,
In song to try, with trembling nerve,
  The limit of its utmost reach,
Only to sound the wretched praise
  Of what to-morrow shall not be,
So mocking with immortal bays
  The cross-bones of mortality!
I do not thus. My faith is fast
  That all the loveliness I sing
Is made to bear the mortal blast,
  And blossom in a better Spring.

The Poet's Humility

From love's abysmal ether rare
  If I to men have here made known

New truths, they, like new stars, were
    there.
  But only not yet written down.
Nor verse, nor art, nor plot, nor plan,
  Nor aught of mine here's worth a toy:
Quit praise and blame, and, if you can,
  Do, brother, for the nonce, enjoy.
Moving but as the feelings move,
  I run, or loiter with delight,
Or stop to mark where gentle Love
  Persuades the soul from height to height.
Yet, know, that, though my words are gay
  As David's dance, which Michael
    scorn'd,
If rightly you peruse the Lay,
  You shall be sweetly help'd and warn'd.

The Impossibility

Of all the impossibilities
  Of love's achieving, surely none
So hopeless as to speak it is.
  By love, in me, may this be done!
Lo, love's obey'd by all. 'Tis right
  That all should know what they obey,
Lest erring conscience damp delight,
  And folly laugh our joys away.
Thou Primal Love, who grantest wings
  And voices to the woodland birds,
Grant me the power of saying things
  Too simple and too sweet for words!

Heaven and Earth

How long shall men deny the flower
  Because its roots are in the earth,
And crave with tears from God the dower
  They have, and have depised as dearth.

THE CATHEDRAL CLOSE

Once more I came to Sarum Close,
  With joy half memory, half desire,
And breathed the sunny wind that rose
  And blew the shadows o'er the Spire,
And toss'd the lilac's scented plumes,
  And sway'd the chestnut's thousand
    cones,

And fill'd my nostrils with perfumes,
   And shaped the clouds in waifs and
      zones,
And wafted down the serious strain
   Of Sarum bells, when, true to time,
I reach'd the Dean's, with heart and brain
   That trembled to the trembling chime.

'Twas half my home six years ago.
   The six years had not alter'd it:
Red-brick and ashlar, long and low,
   With dormers and with oriels lit.
Geranium, lychnis, rose array'd
   The windows, all wide open thrown;
And some one in the Study play'd
   The Wedding-March of Mendelssohn.
And there it was I last took leave:
   'Twas Christmas: I remember'd now
The cruel girls, who feign'd to grieve,
   Took down the evergreens; and how
The laurel into blazes woke
   The fire, lighting the large, low room,
A dim, rich lustre of old oak
   And crimson velvet's glowing gloom.

No change had touch'd Dean Churchill:
      kind,
   By widowhood more than winters bent,
And settled in a cheerful mind,
   As still forecasting heaven's content.
Well might his thoughts be fixed on high,
   Now she was there! Within her face
Humility and dignity
   Were met in a most sweet embrace.
She seem'd expressly sent below
   To teach our erring minds to see
The rhythmic change of time's swift flow
   As part of still eternity.
Her life, all honour, observed, with awe
   Which cross experience could not mar,
The fiction of the Christian law
   That all men honourable are;
And so her smile at once conferr'd
   High flattery and benign reproof;

And I, a rude boy, strangely stirr'd,
   Grew courtly in my own behoof.

Was this her eldest, Honor; prude,
   Who would not let me pull the swing;
Who, kiss'd at Christmas, called me rude,
   And sobb'd alone, and would not sing?
How changed! In shape no slender Grace,
   But Venus; milder than the dove;
Her mother's air; her Norman face;
   Her large sweet eyes, clear lakes of love.
Mary I knew. In former time
   Ailing and pale, she thought that bliss
Was only for a better clime,
   And, heavenly overmuch, scorn'd this.
I, rash with theories of the right,
   Which stretch'd the tether of my Creed,
But did not break it, held delight
   Half discipline. We disagreed.
She told the Dean I wanted grace.
   Now she was kindest of the three,
And two wild roses deck'd her face.
   And, what, was this my Mildred, she
To herself and all a sweet surprise?
   My Pet, who romp'd and roll'd a hoop?
I wonder'd where those daisy eyes
   Had found their touching curve and
      droop.
Unmannerly times! But now we sat
   Stranger than strangers; till I caught
And answer'd Mildred's smile; and that
   Spread to the rest, and freedom brought.
By Honor I was kindly task'd
   To explain my never coming down
From Cambridge; Mary smiled and ask'd
   Were Kant and Goethe yet outgrown?
And, pleased, we talk'd the old days o'er;
   And, parting, I for pleasure sigh'd.
To be there as a friend, (since more!)
   Seem'd then, seems still, excuse for
      pride;
For something that abode endued
   With temple-like repose, an air
Of life's kind purposes pursued
   With order'd freedom sweet and fair.

Mary and Mildred

PRELUDE

The Paragon

When I behold the skies aloft
  Passing the pageantry of dreams,
The cloud whose bosom, cygnet-soft,
  A couch for nuptial Juno seems,
The ocean broad, the mountains bright,
  The shadowy vales with feeding herds,
I from my lyre the music smite,
  Nor want for justly matching words.
All powers of the sea and air,
  All interests of hill and plain,
I so can sing, in seasons fair,
  That who hath felt may feel again;
Nay more, the gracious Muses bless
  At times my tongue until I can,
With moving emphasis, express
  The likeness of the perfect man.
Elated oft by such free songs,
  I think with utterance free to raise
That hymn for which the whole world
    longs,
  A worthy hymn in woman's praise;
A hymn bright-noted like a bird's,
  Arousing these song-sleepy times
With rhapsodies of perfect words,
  Ruled by returning kiss of rhymes.
But when I look on her and hope
  To tell with joy what I admire,
My thoughts lie cramp'd in narrow scope,
  Or in the feeble birth expire;
No skill'd complexity of speech,
  No simple phrase of tenderest fall,
No liken'd excellence can reach
  Her, the most excellent of all.
The best half of creation's best,
  Its heart to feel, its eye to see,
The crown and complex of the rest,
  Its aim and its epitome.
Nay, might I utter my conceit,
  'Twere after all a vulgar song,
For she's so simply, subtly sweet,
  My deepest rapture does her wrong.
Yet it is now my chosen task
  To sing her worth as Maid and Wife;

Nor happier post than this I ask,
  To live her laureate all my life.
On wings of love uplifted free,
  And by her gentleness made great,
I'll teach how noble man should be
  To match with such a lovely mate;
And then in her will move the more
  The woman's wish to be desired,
(By praise increased,) till both shall soar,
  With blissful emulations fired.
And, as geranium, pink, or rose
  Is thrice itself through power of art,
So may my happy skill disclose
  New fairness even in her fair heart;
Until that churl shall nowhere be,
  Who bends not, awed, before the throne
Of her affecting majesty,
  So meek, so far unlike our own;
Until, (for who may hope too much
  From her who wields the powers of
    love?)
Our lifted lives at last shall touch
  That happy goal to which they move;
Until, we find, as darkness rolls
  Away, and evil mists dissolve,
That nuptial contrasts are the poles
  On which the heavenly spheres revolve.

MARY AND MILDRED

One morning, after Church, I walk'd
  Alone with Mary on the Lawn,
And felt myself, howe'er we talk'd,
  To grave themes delicately drawn.
When she, delighted, found I knew
  More of her peace than she supposed,
Our confidences heavenwards grew,
  Like fox-glove buds, in pairs disclosed
Our former faults did we confess,
  Our ancient feud was more than heal'd,
And, with the woman's eagerness
  For amity full-sign'd and seal'd,
She, offering up for sacrifice
  Her heart's reserve, brought out to show
Some verses, made when she was ice
  To all but Heaven, six years ago;
Since happier grown! I took and read
  The neat-writ lines. She, void of guile,

Too late repenting, blush'd, and said,
    I must not think about the style.

.   .   .   .

She from a rose-tree shook the blight;
    And well she knew that I knew well
Her grace with silence to requite.

Honoria

PRELUDE

The Lover

He meets, by heavenly chance express,
    The destined maid; some hidden hand
Unveils to him that loveliness
    Which others cannot understand.
No songs of love, no summer dreams
    Did e'er his longing fancy fire
With vision like to this; she seems
    In all things better than desire!
His merits in her presence grow,
    To match the promise in her eyes,
And round her happy footsteps blow
    The authentic airs of Paradise.
For joy of her he cannot sleep;
    Her beauty haunts him all the night.
It melts his heart, it makes him weep
    For wonder, worship, and delight.

No smallest boon were bought too dear,
    Though barter'd for his love-sick life;
Yet trusts he, with undaunted cheer,
    To vanquish heaven and call her wife.
He notes how queens of sweetness still
    Neglect their crowns, and stoop to mate;
How, self-consign'd with lavish will,
    They ask but love proportionate;
How swift pursuit by small degrees,
    Love's tactic, works like miracle;
How valour, clothed in courtesies,
    Brings down the haughtiest citadel;
And therefore, though he merits not
    To kiss the braid upon her skirt,
His hope, discouraged ne'er a jot,
    Out-soars all possible desert.

The Attainment

You love? That's high as you shall go;
    For 'tis as true as Gospel text,
Not noble then is never so,
    Either in this world or the next.

Honoria

She was all mildness; yet 'twas writ
    Upon her beauty legibly,
'He that's for heaven itself unfit,
    Let him not hope to merit me.'

If question were of her for wife,
    Ill might be mended, hope increased.
Not that I soar'd so far above
    Myself, as this great hope to dare;
And yet I well foresaw that love
    Might hope where reason must despair;
And, half-resenting the sweet pride
    Which would not ask me to admire,
'Oh,' to my secret heart I sigh'd,
    'That I were worthy to desire!'

The Morning Call

PRELUDE

The Rose of the World

Lo, when the Lord made North and South
    And sun and moon ordained, He,
Forthbringing each by word of mouth
    In order of its dignity,
Did man from the crude clay express
    By sequence, and, all else decreed,
He form'd the woman; nor might less
    Than Sabbath such a work succeed.
And still with favour singled out,
    Marr'd less than man by mortal fall,
Her disposition is devout,
    Her countenance angelical;
The best things that the best believe
    Are in her face so kindly writ
The faithless, seeing her, conceive,
    Not only heaven, but hope of it;

No idle thought her instinct shrouds,
   But fancy chequers settled sense,
Like alteration of the clouds
   On noonday's azure permanence;
Pure dignity, composure, ease,
   Declare affections nobly fix'd,
And impulse sprung from due degrees
   Of sense and spirit sweetly mix'd;
Her modesty, her chiefest grace,
   The cestus clasping Venus's side,
Is potent to deject the face
   Of him who would affront its pride;
Wrong dares not in her presence speak,
   Nor spotted thought its taint disclose
Under the protest of a cheek
   Outbragging Nature's boast the rose.
In mind and manners how discreet!
   How artless in her very art;
How candid in discourse; how sweet
   The concord of her lips and heart;
How simple and how circumspect;
   How subtle and how fancy-free;
Though sacred to her love, how deck'd
   With unexclusive courtesy;
How quick in talk to see from far
   The way to vanquish or evade;
How able her persuasions are
   To prove, her reasons to persuade;
How, (not to call true instinct's bent
   And woman's very nature, harm,)
How amiable and innocent
   Her pleasure in her power to charm;
How humbly careful to attract,
   Though crown'd with all the soul
     desires,
Connubial aptitude exact,
   Diversity that never tires.

The Tribute

Boon Nature to the woman bows.
   She walks in all its glory clad,
And, chief herself of earthly shows,
   Each other helps her, and is glad,
No splendour 'neath the sky's proud dome
   But serves for her familiar wear;
The far-fetched diamond finds its home
   Flashing and smouldering in her hair;
For her the seas their pearls reveal;
   Art and strange lands her pomp supply

With purple, chrome, and cochineal,
   Ochre, and lapis lazuli;
The worm its golden woof presents;
   Whatever runs, flies, dives, or delves,
All doff for her their ornaments,
   Which suit her better than themselves;
And all, by this their power to give,
   Proving her right to take, proclaim
Her beauty's clear prerogative
   To profit so by Eden's blame.

Compensation

That nothing here may want its praise,
   Know, she who in her dress reveals
A fine and modest taste, displays
   More loveliness than she conceals.

THE MORNING CALL

'Full many a lady has ere now
   My apprehensive fancy fired,
And woven many a transient chain;
   But never lady like to this,
Who holds me as the weather-vane
   Is held by yonder clematis.
She seems the life of nature's powers;
   Her beauty is the genial thought
Which makes the sunshine bright; the
     flowers,
   But for their hint of her, were nought.'
A voice, the sweeter for the grace
   Of suddenness, while thus I dream'd,
'Good morning!' said or sang. Her face
   The mirror of the morning seem'd.
Her sisters in the garden walk'd,
   And would I come? Across the Hall
She took me; and we laugh'd and talk'd
   About the Flower-show and the Ball.
The sweet hour lapsed, and left my breast
   A load of joy and tender care;
And this delight, which life oppress'd,
   To fix'd aims grew, that ask'd for pray'r.

I went, and closed and lock'd the door,
And cast myself down on my bed,
   And there, with many a blissful tear,
I vow'd to love and pray'd to wed
   The maiden who had grown so dear;

Thank'd God who had set her in my path;
  And promised, as I hoped to win,
I never would sully my faith
  By the least selfishness or sin.

The Violets

PRELUDE

The Parallel

I know not how to her it seems,
  Or how to a perfect judging eye,
But, as my loving thought esteems,
  Man misdeserves his sweet ally.
Where she succeeds with cloudless brow,
  In common and in holy course,
He fails, in spite of prayer and vow
  And agonies of faith and force;
Or, if his suit with Heaven prevails
  To righteous life, his virtuous deeds
Lack beauty, virtue's badge; she fails
  More graciously than he succeeds.
Her spirit, compact of gentleness,
  If Heaven postpones or grants her
     prayer,
Conceives no pride in its success,
  And in its failure no despair.

Prospective Faith

They safely walk in darkest ways
  Whose youth is lighted from above,
Where, through the senses' silvery haze,
  Dawns the veil'd moon of nuptial love.
Who is the happy husband? He
  Who, scanning his unwedded life,
Thanks Heaven, with a conscience free,
  'Twas faithful to his future wife.

THE VIOLETS

I went not to the Dean's unbid,
  For I'd not have my mystery,
From her so delicately hid,
  Discuss'd by gossips at their tea.
A long, long week, and not once there,
  Had made my spirit sick and faint,

And lack-love, foul as love is fair,
  Perverted all things to complaint.
How vain the world had grown to be!
  How mean all people and their ways,
How ignorant their sympathy,
  And how impertinent their praise;
To my necessity how strange
  The sunshine and the song of birds;
How dull the clouds' continual change,
  How foolishly content the herds;
How unaccountable the law
  Which bade me sit in blindness here,
While she, the sun by which I saw,
  Shed splendour in an idle sphere!
And then I kiss'd her stolen glove,
  And sigh'd to reckon and define
The modes of martyrdom in love,
  And how far each one might be mine.
Wretched were life, if the end were now!
  But this gives tears to dry despair,
Faith shall be blest, we know not how,
  And love fulfill'd, we know not where.

While thus I grieved, and kiss'd her glove,
  My man brought in her note to say,
Papa had bid her send his love,
  And would I dine with them next day?
They had learn'd and practised Purcell's
    glee,
  To sing it by to-morrow night.
The Postscript was: Her sisters and she
  Inclosed some violets, blue and white;
She and her sisters found them where
  I wager'd once no violets grew;
So they had won the gloves. And there
  The violets lay, two white, one blue.

The Dean

PRELUDE

Perfect Love rare

Most rare is still most noble found,
  Most noble still most incomplete;
Sad law, which leaves King Love
    uncrown'd
  In this obscure, terrestrial seat!

With bale more sweet than others' bliss,
　　And bliss more wise than others' bale,
The secrets of the world are his,
　　And freedom without let or pale.

Love Justified

This little germ of nuptial love,
　　Which springs so simply from the sod,
The root is, as my song shall prove,
　　Of all our love to man and God.

Love Serviceable

What measure Fate to him shall mete
　　Is not the noble Lover's care;
He's heart-sick with a longing sweet
　　To make her happy as she's fair.
And, holding life as so much pelf
　　To buy her posies, learns this lore:
He does not rightly love himself
　　Who does not love another more.

Love a Virtue

Strong passions mean weak will, and he
　　Who truly knows the strength and bliss
Which are in love, will own with me
　　No passion but a virtue 'tis.
Ice-cold strikes heaven's noble glow
　　To spirits whose vital heat is hell;
And to corrupt hearts even so
　　The songs I sing, the tale I tell.
These cannot see the robes of white
　　In which I sing of love. Alack,
But darkness shows in heavenly light,
　　Though whiteness, in the dark, is black!

THE DEAN

The Ladies rose. I held the door,
　　And sigh'd, as her departing grace
Assured me that she alway wore
　　A heart as happy as her face;

Towards my mark the Dean's talk set:
　　He praised my 'Notes on Abury,'
Read when the Association met
　　At Sarum; he was glad to see

I had not stopp'd, as some men had,
　　At Wrangler and Prize Poet; last,
He hoped the business was not bad
　　I came about: then the wine pass'd.

A full glass prefaced my reply:
　　I loved his daughter, Honor; he knew
My estate and prospects; might I try
　　To win her? To mine eyes tears flew.
He thought 'twas that. I might. He gave
　　His true consent, if I could get
Her love. A dear, good Girl! she'd have
　　Only three thousand pounds as yet;
More bye and bye. Yes, his good will
　　Should go with me; he would not stir;
He and my father in old time still
　　Wish'd I should one day marry her;
That, though his blessing and his prayer
　　Had help'd, should help, my suit, yet he
Left all to me, his passive share
　　Consent and opportunity.
My chance, he hoped, was good: I'd won
　　Some name already; friends and place
Appear'd within my reach, but none
　　Her mind and manners would not grace.

Ætna and the Moon

PRELUDE

The Prodigal

To heroism and holiness
　　How hard it is for man to soar
But how much harder to be less
　　Than what his mistress loves him for!
There is no man so full of pride,
　　And none so intimate with shame,
And none to manhood so denied,
　　As not to mend if women blame.
He does with ease what do he must,
　　Or merit this, and nought's debarr'd
From man, when woman shall be just
　　In yielding her desired regard.
Ah, wasteful woman, she who may
　　On her sweet self set her own price,
Knowing he cannot choose but pay,
　　How has she cheapen'd paradise;

How given for nought her priceless gift,
  How spoil'd the bread and spill'd the
    wine,
Which, spent with due, respective thrift,
  Had made brutes men, and men divine.

The Metamorphosis

Maid, choosing man, remember this:
  You take his nature with his name.
Ask, too, what his religion is,
  For you will soon be of the same.

ÆTNA AND THE MOON

To ease my heart, I feigning, seized
  A pen, and, showering tears, declared
My unfeign'd passion; sadly pleased
  Only to dream that so I dared.
Thus was the fervid truth confess'd,
  But wild with paradox ran the plea,
As wilfully in hope depress'd,
  Yet bold beyond hope's warranty:

'O, more than dear, be more than just,
  And do not deafly shut the door!
I claim no right to speak; I trust
  Mercy, not right; yet who has more?
Your name pronounced brings to my heart
  A feeling like the violet's breath,
Which does so much of heaven impart
  It makes me yearn with tears for death;
The winds that in the garden toss
  The Guelder-roses give me pain,
Alarm me with the dread of loss,
  Exhaust me with the dream of gain;
I'm troubled by the clouds that move;
  Thrill'd by the breath which I respire;
And ever, like a torch, my love,
  Thus agitated, flames the higher;
All's hard that has not you for goal;
  I scarce can move my hand to write,
For love engages all my soul,
  And leaves the body void of might;
The wings of will spread idly as do
  The bird's that in a vacuum lies;

My breast, asleep with dreams of you,
  Forgets to breathe, and bursts in sighs;
I see no rest this side the grave,
  No rest or hope from you apart;
Your life is in the rose you gave,
  Its perfume suffocates my heart;
There's no refreshment in the breeze;
  The heaven o'erwhelms me with its blue;
I faint beside the dancing seas;
  Winds, skies, and waves are only you;
The thought or act which not intends
  You service, seems a sin and shame;
In that one only object ends
  Conscience, religion, honour, fame.
Yet think not, Dear, that, thus engaged,
  These drop their heavenly function; no,
They simply bow where Heaven's
    presaged
In semblance of the liveliest show.
Ah, could I put off love! Could we
  Never have met! What calm, what ease
Nay, but, alas, this remedy
  Were ten times worse than the disease;
For when, indifferent, I pursue
  The world's best pleasures for relief,
My heart, still sickening back to you,
  Finds none like memory of its grief;
And, though 'twere very hell to hear
  You felt such misery as I,
All good, save you, were far less dear
  Than is that ill with which I die!
Where'er I go, wandering forlorn,
  You are the world's love, life and glee:
O, wretchedness not to be borne
  If she that's Love should not love me!'

I could not write another word,
  Through pity for my own distress;
And forth I went, untimely stirr'd
  To make my misery more or less.
I went, beneath the heated noon,
  To where, in her simplicity,
She sat at work; and, as the Moon
  On Ætna smiles, she smiled on me;
But, now and then, in cheek and eyes,
  I saw, or fancied, such a glow
As when, in summer-evening skies,
Some say 'It lightens,' some say 'No.'

Sarum Plain

PRELUDE

The Revelation

An idle poet, here and there,
  Looks round him, but, for all the rest,
The world, unfathomably fair,
  Is duller than a witling's jest.
Love wakes men, once a life-time each;
  They lift their heavy lids, and look;
And, lo, what one sweet page can teach
  They read with joy, then shut the book.
And some give thanks, and some
    blaspheme,
  And most forget; but, either way,
That and the Child's unheeded dream
  Is all the light of all their day.

The Spirit's Epochs

Not in the crises of events,
  Of compass'd hopes, or fears fulfill'd,
Or acts of gravest consequence,
  Are life's delight and depth reveal'd.
I drew my bride, beneath the moon,
  Across my threshold; happy hour!
But, ah, the walk that afternoon
  We saw the water-flags in flower!

The Prototype

Lo, there, whence love, life, light are
    pour'd,
  Veil'd with impenetrable rays,
Amidst the presence of the Lord
  Co-equal Wisdom laughs and plays.
Female and male God made the man;
  His image is the whole, not half;
And in our love we dimly scan
  The love which is between Himself.

SARUM PLAIN

Brief worship done, which still endows
  The day with beauty not its own;
Breakfast enjoy'd, 'mid hush of boughs
  And perfumes thro' the windows blown;

With intervening pause, that paints
  Each act with honour, life with calm,
(As old processions of the Saints
  At every step have wands of palm),
We rose; the ladies went to dress,
  And soon return'd with smiles; and then,
Plans fix'd, to which the Dean said Yes,
  Once more we drove to Salisbury Plain.
We past my house, (observed with praise
  By Mildred, Mary acquiesced),
And left the old and lazy greys
  Below the hill, and walk'd the rest.
The moods of love are like the wind,
  And none knows whence or why they
    rise,
I ne'er before felt heart and mind
  So much affected through mine eyes.
How cognate with the flatter'd air,
  How form'd for earth's familiar zone,
She moved; how feeling and how fair
  For others' pleasure and her own;
And, ah, the heaven of her face!
  How, when she laugh'd, I seem'd to see
The gladness of the primal grace,
  And how, when grave, its dignity!
Of all she was, the least not less
  Delighted the devoted eye;
No fold or fashion of her dress
  Her fairness did not sanctify;
Better it seem'd as now to walk,
  And humbly by her gentle side
Observe her smile and hear her talk,
  Then call the world's next best my bride.

By the great stones we chose our ground
  For shade; and there, in converse sweet,
Took luncheon. On a little mound
  Sat the three ladies; at their feet,
I sat; and smelt the heathy smell,
  Pluck'd hare-bells, turn'd the telescope
To the country round. My life went well,
  For once, without the wheels of hope;
And I despised the Druid rocks
  That scowled their chill gloom from
    above,
Like churls whose stolid wisdom mocks
  The lightness of immortal love.
And, as we talk'd, my spirit quaff'd
  The sparkling winds; the candid skies

At our untruthful strangeness laugh'd;
   I kiss'd with mine her smiling eyes;
And sweet familiarness and awe
   Prevail'd that hour on either part.

Sahara

PRELUDE

The Wife's Tragedy

Man must be pleased; but him to please
   Is woman's pleasure; down the gulf
Of his condoled necessities
   She casts her best, she flings herself.
How often flings for nought! and yokes
   Her heart to an icicle or whim,
Whose each impatient word provokes
   Another, not from her, but him;
While she, too gentle even to force
   His penitence by kind replies,
Waits by, expecting his remorse,
   With pardon in her pitying eyes;
And if he once, by shame oppress'd,
   A comfortable word confers,
She leans and weeps against his breast,
   And seems to think the sin was hers;
And whilst his love has any life,
   Or any eye to see her charms,
At any time, she's still his wife,
   Dearly devoted to his arms;
She loves with love that cannot tire;
   And when, ah woe, she loves alone,
Through passionate duty love flames
    higher,
   As grass grows taller round a stone.

Common Graces

O man, (and Legion is thy name,)
   Who hadst for dowry with thy wife
A conduct void of outward blame,
   The beauty of a loyal life,
Is nature in thee too spiritless,
   Ignoble, impotent, and dead,
To prize her love and loveliness

The more for being thy daily bread?
And art thou one of that vile crew
   Which see no splendour in the sun,
Praising alone the good that's new,
   Or over, or not yet begun?
And has it dawn'd on thy dull wits
   That love warms many as soft a nest,
That, though swathed round with benefits,
   Thou art not singularly blest?
And fail thy thanks for gifts divine,
   The common food of many a heart,
Because they are not only thine?
   Beware lest in the end thou art
Cast as a goat forth from the fold,
   Too proud to feel the common grace
Of blissful myriads who behold
   For evermore the Father's face.

SAHARA

I stood by Honor and the Dean,
   They seated in the London train.
A month from her! yet this had been,
   Ere now, without such bitter pain.
But neighbourhood makes parting light,
   And distance remedy has none;
Alone, she near, I felt as might
   A blind man sitting in the sun;
She near, all for the time was well;
   Hope's self, when we were far apart,
With lonely feeling, like the smell
   Of heath on mountains, fill'd my heart.

The bell rang, and, with shrieks like death,
   Link catching link, the long array,
With ponderous pulse and fiery breath,
   Proud of its burthen, swept away;
And through the lingering crowd I broke,
   Sought the hill-side, and thence,
    heart-sick,
Beheld, far off, the little smoke
   Along the landscape kindling quick.
Life without her was vain and gross,
   The glory from the world was gone,
And on the gardens of the Close
   As on Sahara shone the sun.

Going to Church

I woke at three; for I was bid
   To breakfast with the Dean at nine,
And thence to Church. My curtain slid,
   I found the dawning Sunday fine.

My prayers for her being done, I took
   Occasion by the quiet hour
To find and know, by Rule and Book,
   The rights of love's beloved power.

My giddiest hope allow'd
No selfish thought, or earthly smirch;
And forth I went, in peace, and proud
   To take my passion into Church.
I found them, with exactest grace
   And fresh as Spring, for Spring attired;
And by the radiance in her face
   I saw she felt she was admired;
And, through the common luck of love,
   A moment's fortunate delay,
To fit the little lilac glove,
   Gave me her arm; and I and they,
(They true to this and every hour,
   As if attended on by Time),
Went into Church while yet the tower
   Was noisy with the finish'd chime.

Her soft voice, singularly heard
   Beside me, in the Psalms, withstood
The roar of voices, like a bird
   Sole warbling in a windy wood;
And, when we knelt, she seem'd to be
   An angel teaching me to pray;
And all through the high Liturgy
   My spirit rejoiced without allay.

The Dance

PRELUDE

The Daughter of Eve

The woman's gentle mood o'er-stept
   Withers my love, that lightly scans
The rest, and does in her accept
   All her own faults, but none of man's.

As man I cannot judge her ill,
   Or honour her fair station less,
Who with a woman's errors, still
   Preserves a woman's gentleness.

Aurea Dicta

Child, would you shun the vulgar doom,
   In love disgust, in death despair?
Know, death must come and love must
   come,
   And so for each your soul prepare.

Lest sacred love your soul ensnare,
   With pious fancy still infer
'How loving and how lovely fair
   Must he be who has fashioned her!'

Love's perfect blossom only blows
   Where noble manners veil defect.
Angels may be familiar; those
   Who err each other must respect.

Love blabb'd of is a great decline;
   A careless word unsanctions sense;
But he who casts Heaven's truth to swine
   Consummates all incontinence.

THE DANCE

'My memory of heaven awakes!
   She's not of the earth, although her light,
As lantern'd by her body, makes
   A piece of it past bearing bright.
So innocently proud and fair
   She is, that Wisdom sings for glee
And Folly dies, breathing one air
   With such a bright-cheek'd chastity;
And though her charms are a strong law
   Compelling all men to admire,
They go so clad with lovely awe
   None but the noble dares desire.'

This learn'd I, watching where she danced,
   Native to melody and light,
And now and then toward me glanced,
   Pleased, as I hoped, to please my sight.

Ah, love to speak was impotent,
　　Till music did a tongue confer,
And I ne'er knew what music meant,
　　Until I danced to it with her.
I press'd her hand, by will or chance
　　I know not, but I saw the rays
Withdrawn, which did till then enhance
　　Her fairness with its thanks for praise.
I knew my spirit's vague offence
　　Was patent to the dreaming eye
And heavenly tact of innocence,
　　And did for fear my fear defy,
And ask'd her for the next dance.
　　'Yes.'

I saw she saw; and, O sweet Heaven,
　　Could my glad mind have credited
That influence had to me been given
　　To affect her so, I should have said
That, though she from herself conceal'd
　　Love's felt delight and fancied harm,
They made her face the jousting field
　　Of joy and beautiful alarm.

The Abdication

From little signs, like little stars,
　　Whose faint impression on the sense
The very looking straight at mars,
　　Or only seen by confluence;
From instinct of a mutual thought,
　　Whence sanctity of manners flow'd;
From chance unconscious, and from what
　　Concealment, overconscious, show'd;
Her hand's less weight upon my arm,
　　Her lowlier mien; that match'd with this;
I found, and felt with strange alarm,
　　I stood committed to my bliss.

I grew assur'd, before I ask'd,
　　That she'd be mine without reserve,
And in her unclaim'd graces bask'd,
　　At leisure, till the time should serve,
With just enough of dread to thrill
　　The hope, and make it trebly dear;
Thus loth to speak the word to kill
　　Either the hope or happy fear.

Till once, through lanes returning late,
　　Her laughing sisters lagg'd behind;
And, ere we reach'd her father's gate,
　　We paused with one presentient mind;
And, in the dim and perfumed mist,
　　Their coming stay'd, who, friends to
　　　me,
And very women, loved to assist
　　Love's timid opportunity.

Twice rose, twice died my trembling
　　　word;
　　The faint and frail Cathedral chimes
Spake time in music, and we heard
　　The chafers rustling in the limes.
Her dress, that touch'd me where I stood,
　　The warmth of her confided arm,
Her bosom's gentle neighbourhood,
　　Her pleasure in her power to charm;
Her look, her love, her form, her touch,
　　The least seem'd most by blissful turn,
Blissful but that it pleased too much,
　　And taught the wayward soul to yearn.
It was as if a harp with wires
　　Was traversed by the breath I drew;
And, oh, sweet meeting of desires,
　　She, answering, own'd that she loved
　　　too.

Honoria was to be my bride!
　　The hopeless heights of hope were
　　　scaled;
The summit won, I paused and sigh'd,
　　As if success itself had fail'd.
It seem'd as if my lips approach'd
　　To touch at Tantalus' reward,
And rashly on Eden life encroach'd,
　　Half-blinded by the flaming sword.
The whole world's wealthiest and its best,
　　So fiercely sought, appear'd, when
　　　found,
Poor in its need to be possess'd,
　　Poor from its very want of bound.
By that consenting scared and shock'd,
　　Such change came o'er her mien and
　　　mood
That I felt startled and half-mock'd,
　　As winning what I had not woo'd.

My queen was crouching at my side,
    By love unscepter'd and brought low,
Her awful garb of maiden pride
    All melted into tears like snow;
The mistress of my reverent thought,
    Whose praise was all I ask'd of fame,
In my close-watch'd approval sought
    Protection as from danger and blame;
Her soul, which late I loved to invest
    With pity for my poor desert,
Buried its face within my breast,
    Like a pet fawn by hunters hurt.

Book II

Accepted

What fortune did my heart foretell?
    What shook my spirit, as I woke,
Like the vibration of a bell
    Of which I had not heard the stroke?
Was it some happy vision shut
    From memory by the sun's fresh ray?
Was it that linnet's song; or but
    A natural gratitude for day?
Or the mere joy the senses weave,
    A wayward ecstasy of life?
Then I remember'd, yester-eve
    I won Honoria for my wife.

The Course of True Love

PRELUDE

The Changed Allegiance

Watch how a bird, that captived sings,
    The cage set open, first looks out,
Yet fears the freedom of his wings,
    And now withdraws, and flits about,
The maiden so, from love's free sky
    In chaste and prudent counsels caged,
But longing to be loosen'd by
    Her suitor's faith declared and gaged,

When blest with that release desired,
    First doubts if truly she is free,
Then pauses, restlessly retired,
    Alarm'd at too much liberty;
But after that, habitual faith,
    Divorced from self, where late 'twas
        due,
Walks nobly in its novel path,
    And she's to changed allegiance true;
And, prizing what she can't prevent,
    (Right wisdom, often misdeem'd
        whim,)
Her will's indomitably bent
    On mere submissiveness to him;
To him she'll cleave, for him forsake
    Father's and mother's fond command!
He is her lord, for he can take
    Hold of her faint heart with his hand.

THE COURSE OF TRUE LOVE

Oh, beating heart of sweet alarm,
    Which stays the lover's step when near
His mistress and her awful charm
    Of grace and innocence sincere!
I held the half-shut door and heard
    The voice of my betrothed wife,
Who sang my verses, every word
    By music taught its latent life.

    .   .   .   .

'Go, Child, and see him out yourself,'
    The Dean said, after tea, 'and shew
The place, upon that upper shelf,
    Where Tasso stands, lent long ago.'

A rose in ruin, from her breast,
    Fell, as I took a fond adieu,
'These rose-leaves to my heart be press'd,
    Honoria, while it aches for you!'
'You must go now, Love!' 'See, the air
    Is thick with starlight!' 'Let me tie
This scarf on. Oh, your Tasso! There!
    I'm coming, Aunt!' 'Sweet, Sweet!'
        'Good-bye!'
With love's bright arrows from her eyes,
    And balm on her permissive lips,
She pass'd, and night was a surprise,
    As when the sun at Quito dips.

The County Ball

PRELUDE

Love Ceremonious

Keep your undrest, familiar style
  For strangers, but respect your friend,
Her most, whose matrimonial smile
  Is and asks honour without end.
'Tis found, and needs it must so be,
  That life from love's allegiance flags,
When love forgets his majesty
  In sloth's unceremonious rags.
Let love make home a gracious Court;
  There let the world's rude, hasty ways
Be fashion'd to a loftier port,
  And learn to bow and stand at gaze;
And let the sweet, respective sphere
  Of personal worship there obtain
Circumference for moving clear,
  None treading on another's train.
This makes that pleasures do not cloy,
  And dignifies our mortal strife
With calmness and considerate joy,
  Befitting our immortal life.

THE COUNTY BALL

Well, Heaven be thank'd my first-love
    fail'd,
  As, Heaven be thank'd, our first-loves
    do!
Thought I, when Fanny past me sail'd,
  Loved once, for what I never knew.

But there danced she, who from the leaven
  Of ill preserved my heart and wit
All unawares, for she was heaven,
  Others at best but fit for it.
One of those lovely things she was
  In whose least action there can be
Nothing so transient but it has
  An air of immortality.
Her motion, feeling 'twas beloved,
  The pensive soul of tune express'd,
And, oh, what perfume, as she moved,
  Came from the flowers in her breast!

Ah, none but I discern'd her looks,
  When in the throng she pass'd me by,
For love is like a ghost, and brooks
  Only the chosen seer's eye.
Whilst so her beauty fed my sight,
  And whilst I lived in what she said,
Accordant airs, like all delight
  Most sweet when noted least, were
    play'd;
I held my breath, and thought 'how
    bright!'
That guileless beauty in its noon,
Compelling tribute of desires
  Ardent as day when Sirius reigns,
Pure as the permeating fires
  That smoulder in the opal's veins.

The Koh-i-Noor

PRELUDE

Love Thinking

What lifts her in my thought so far
  Beyond all else? Let Love not err!
'Tis that which all right women are,
  But which I'll know in none but her.
She is to me the only Ark
  Of that high mystery which locks
The lips of joy, or speaks in dark
  Enigmas and in paradox;
That potent charm, which none can fly,
  Nor would, which makes me bond and
    free,
Nor can I tell if first 'twas I
  Chose it, or it elected me.

THE KOH-I-NOOR

'Be man's hard virtues highly wrought,
  But let my gentle Mistress be,
In every look, word, deed, and thought,
  Nothing but sweet and womanly!
Her virtues please my virtuous mood,
  But what at all times I admire
Is, not that she is wise or good,
  But just the thing which I desire.

With versatility to bring
    Her mental tone to any strain,
If oft'nest she is anything,
    Be it thoughtless, talkative, and vain.
That seems in her supremest grace
    Which, virtue or not, apprises me
That my familiar thoughts embrace
    Unfathomable mystery.'

I answer'd thus; for she desired
    To know what mind I most approved
Partly to learn what she inquired,
    Partly to get the praise she loved.
I praised her, but no praise could fill
    The depths of her desire to please,
Though dull to others as a Will
    To them that have no legacies.
The more I praised the more she shone,
    Her eyes incredulously bright,
And all her happy beauty blown
    Beneath the beams of my delight.
Sweet rivalry was thus begot;
    By turns, my speech, in passion's style,
With flatteries the truth o'ershot,
    And she surpass'd them with her smile.

'Dear Felix!' 'Sweet, sweet Love!' But there
    Was Aunt Maude's noisy ring and
        knock!
'Stay, Felix; you have caught my hair.
    Stoop! Thank you!' 'May I have that
        lock?'
'Not now. Good morning, Aunt!' 'Why,
        Puss,
    'You look magnificent to-day.'
'Here's Felix, Aunt.' 'Fox and green goose!
    Who handsome gets should handsome
        pay.'
'Aunt, you are friends!' 'Ah, to be sure!
    Good morning! Go on flattering, Sir;
A woman's like the Koh-i-noor,
    Worth just the price that's put on her.'

The Epitaph

PRELUDE

The Last Night at Home

Oh, Muse, who dost to me reveal
    The mystery of the woman's life,
Relate how 'tis a maid might feel,
    The night before she's crown'd a wife!
Lo, sleepless in her little bed,
    She lies and counts the hours till noon.
Ere this, to-morrow, she'll be wed,
    Ere this? Alas, how strangely soon!
A fearful blank of ignorance
    Lies manifest across her way,
And shadows, cast from unknown chance,
    Make sad and dim the coming day.
Her faithless dread she now discards,
    And now remorseful memory flings
Its glory round the last regards
    Of home and all accustom'd things.
Her father's voice, her mother's eyes
    Accuse her treason; 'tis in vain
She thinks herself a wife, and tries
    To comprehend the greater gain;
Her unknown fortune nothing cheers
    Her loving heart's familiar loss,
And torrents of repentant tears
    Their hot and smarting threshold cross.
When first within her bosom Love
    Took birth, and beat his blissful wings,
It seem'd to lift her mind above
    All care for other earthly things;
But, oh, too lightly did she vow
    To leave for aye her happy nest;
And dreadful is the thought that now
    Assaults her weak and shaken breast:
Ah, should her lover's love abate;
    Ah, should she, miserable, lose
All dear regards of maiden state,
    Dissolved by time and marriage dues!
And so her fears increase, till fear
    O'erfilms her apprehensive eye
That she may swoon, with no one near,
    And haply so, unmarried, die.
With instinct of her ignorance,
    (The virgin's strength and veiled guide,)

She prays, and casts the reins of chance
　To Love, nor recks what shall betide.

． ． ． ． ．

The gentle wife, who decks his board
　And makes his day to have no night,
Whose wishes wait upon her lord,
　Who finds her own in his delight,
Is she another now than she
　Who, mistress of her maiden charms,
At his wild prayer, incredibly
　Committed them to his proud arms?
Unless her choice of him's a slur
　Which makes her proper credit dim,
He never enough can honour her
　Who past all speech has honour'd him.

The Foreign Land

A woman is a foreign land,
　Of which, though there he settle young
A man will ne'er quite understand
　The customs, politics, and tongue.
The foolish hie them post-haste through,
　See fashions odd, and prospects fair,
Learn of the language, 'How-d'ye do,'
　And go and brag that they've been there.
The most for leave to trade apply,
　For once, at Empire's seat her heart,
Then get what knowledge ear and eye
　Glean chancewise in the life-long mart.
And certain others few and fit,
　Attach them to the Court, and see
The Country's best, its accent hit,
　And partly sound its polity.

THE EPITAPH

'At Church in twelve hours more, we
　　meet!
　This Dearest, is our last farewell.'
'Oh, Felix, do you love me?' 'Sweet,
　Why do you ask?' 'I cannot tell.'

And was it no vain fantasy
　That raised me from the earth with
　　pride?
Should I to-morrow verily
　Be Bridegroom, and Honoria Bride?

Should I, in simple fact, henceforth
　Live unconditionally lord
Of her whose smile for brightest worth
　Seem'd all too bountiful reward?
If now to part with her could make
　Her pleasure greater, sorrow less,
I for my epitaph would take
　'To serve seem'd more than to possess.'
And I perceived, (the vision sweet
　Dimming with happy dew mine eyes,)
That love and joy are torches lit
　From altar-fires of sacrifice.

Across the sky the daylight crept,
　And birds grew garrulous in the grove,
And on my marriage-morn I slept
　A soft sleep, undisturb'd by love.

The Wedding

PRELUDE

Constancy rewarded

I vow'd unvarying faith, and she,
　To whom in full I pay that vow,
Rewards me with variety
　Which men who change can never
　　know.

THE WEDDING

Life smitten with a feverish chill,
　The brain too tired to understand,
In apathy of heart and will,
　I took the woman from the hand
Of him who stood for God, and heard
　Of Christ, and of the Church his Bride;
The Feast, by presence of the Lord
　And his first Wonder, beautified;
The mystic sense to Christian men;
　The bonds in innocency made,
And gravely to be enter'd then
　For children, godliness, and aid,
And honour'd, and kept free from smirch;
　And how a man must love his wife

No less than Christ did love his Church,
 If need be, giving her his life;
And, vowing then the mutual vow,
 The tongue spake, but intention slept.
'Tis well for us Heaven asks not how
 This oath is sworn, but how 'tis kept.

O, bold seal of a bashful bond,
 Which makes the marriage-day to be,
To those before it and beyond,
 An ice-berg in an Indian sea!

'Now, while she's changing,' said the
  Dean,
 'Her bridal for her travelling dress,
I'll preach allegiance to your queen!
 Preaching's the trade which I profess;
And one more minute's mine! You know
 I've paid my girl a father's debt,
And this last charge is all I owe.
 She's yours; but I love more than yet
You can; such fondness only wakes
 When time has raised the heart above
The prejudice of youth, which makes
 Beauty conditional to love.
Prepare to meet the weak alarms
 Of novel nearness; recollect
The eye which magnifies her charms
 Is microscopic for defect.
Fear comes at first; but soon, rejoiced,
 You'll find your strong and tender loves
Like holy rocks by Druids poised,
 The least force shakes, but none
  removes.
Although you smile, there's much to
  mend!
 Yet never girl, I think, had less.
Her worst point is, she's apt to spend
 Too much on alms-deeds and on dress.
Her strength is your esteem; beware
 Of finding fault; her will's unnerv'd
By blame; from you 'twould be despair;
 But praise that is not quite deserv'd
Will all her noble nature move
 To make your utmost wishes true.
Yet think, while mending thus your Love,
 Of matching her ideal too!
The death of nuptial joy is sloth:
 To keep your mistress in your wife,

Keep to the very height your oath,
 And honour her with arduous life.
Lastly, no personal reverence doff.
 Life's all externals unto those
Who pluck the blushing petals off,
 To find the secret of the rose. –
How long she's staying! Green's Hotel
 I'm sure you'll like. The charge is fair,
The wines good. I remember well
 I stopp'd once, with her mother, there.
A tender conscience of her vow
 That mother had! She is so like her!'
But Mrs Fife, much flurried, now
 Whisper'd, 'Miss Honor's ready, Sir.'

Husband and Wife

PRELUDE

The Married Lover

Why, having won her, do I woo?
 Because her spirit's vestal grace
Provokes me always to pursue,
 But, spirit-like, eludes embrace;
Because her womanhood is such
 That, as on court-days subjects kiss
The Queen's hand, yet so near a touch
 Affirms no mean familiarness,
Because although in act and word
 As lowly as a wife can be,
Her manners, when they call me Lord,
 Remind me 'tis by courtesy;
Because, though free of the outer court
 I am, this Temple keeps its shrine
Sacred to Heaven; because, in short,
 She's not and never shall be mine.

HUSBAND AND WIFE

As souls, ambitious, but low-born,
 If raised past hope by luck or wit,
All pride of place will proudly scorn,
 And live as they'd been used to it,
So we two wore our strange estate;
 Familiar, unaffected, free,

We talk'd, until the dusk grew late,
  Of this and that; but, after tea,
As doubtful if a lot so sweet
  As ours was ours in very sooth,
Like children, to promote conceit,
  We feign'd that it was not the truth;
And she assumed the maiden coy,
  And I adored remorseless charms,
And then we clapp'd our hands for joy
  And ran into each other's arms.

The Epilogue

'Ah, dearest wife, a fresh-lit fire
  Sends forth to heaven great shows of
    fume,
And watchers, far away, admire;
  But when the flames their power
    assume,
The more they burn the less they show,
  The clouds no longer smirch the sky,
And then the flames intensest glow

When far-off watchers think they die.
The fumes of early love my verse
  Has figured –' 'You must paint the
    flame!'
''Twould merit the Promethean curse!
  But now, Sweet, for your praise and
    blame.'
'You speak too boldly; veils are due
  To women's feelings,' 'Fear not this!
Women will vow I say not true,
  And men believe the lips they kiss.'
'I did not call you "Dear" or "Love,"
  I think, till after Frank was born.'
'That fault I cannot well remove;
  The rhymes' – but Frank now blew his
    horn,
And Walter bark'd on hands and knees,
  At Baby in the mignonette,
And all made, full-cry, for the trees
  Where Felix and his wife were set.
Again disturb'd, (crickets have cares!)
  True to their annual use they rose,
To offer thanks at Evening Prayers
  In three times sacred Sarum Close.

APPENDIX B

Portraits of Dr Andrews

DATE	MEDIUM	ARTIST	LOCATION	NOTES
1819?	Oil painting	Wm. Hudson	Unknown	Perhaps item 6565 in a typed inventory in the Cuming Museum, Walworth, London: 'The Rev. Dr. Andrews. Portrait in oil'. Now missing, thought to have been destroyed by enemy action during the 2nd World War.
1820	Engraving	E. Scriven	Family archives, England. (Miss Bastian's scrapbook.)	This is an engraving of the 1819(?) painting by Hudson noted above. The only known copy is marked 'Proof', so perhaps it was never published.
1824	Miniature oil painting on ivory	Wm. Hudson	Family archives, Australia: Mrs Rennie's collection	Exhibited at the Royal Academy, 1825, Cat. No. 854. Signed: '1824 W. Hudson'.
1825?	Engraving	Unknown	No copy traced	Referred to in *Southwark Men of Mark* p. 6, by R. W. Mould, 1905. 'There is an engraving of Dr. Andrews visiting a condemned cell.' This was probably made after the execution of William Probert in 1825 which Dr Andrews attended and which attracted some prominence. See p. 15.

DATE	MEDIUM	ARTIST	LOCATION	NOTES
Post 1824	Engraving	R. Fenner	National Portrait Gallery, London	This is an engraving of the 1824 miniature by Hudson, noted above.
Undated	Engraving	S. Watts	Family archives, Australia: Mrs Rennie's collection	Inscribed: 'G. Patten Pinxt' 'S. Watts Sculpt'. Location of original is unknown.
1826?	Painting	J. Lonsdale	Unknown	Perhaps item 6565 in a typed inventory in the Cuming Museum, Walworth, London. See first item in this list.
1827	Engraving	R. J. Lane	National Portrait Gallery, London	Published by Ebenezer Palmer, London. This is an engraving of the 1826? painting by Lonsdale, noted above.
1827?	Painting	J. R. Wildman	Unknown	Perhaps item 6565 in a typed inventory in the Cuming Museum, Walworth, London. See first item in this list.
1828	Engraving	G. Parker	*Evangelical Magazine*, June, 1828 (Evangelical Library, London)	This is an engraving of the 1827? painting by Wildman, noted above.
1841	Engraving	Unknown	*Gospel Magazine*, February, 1841 (Evangelical Library, London)	The year of Dr Andrews' death.
c. 1840?	Bust, plaster	Unknown	Cuming Museum, Walworth, London	Item 6529, typed inventory.

Source Notes

All quotations are from the first editions of the different books of *The Angel in the House*: 'The Betrothal' 1854, 'The Espousals' 1856, 'Faithful For Ever' 1860, 'Victories Of Love' 1863. The poem was last published as a whole in 1905.

The following abbreviations have been used in the notes and references at the end of each chapter.

FULL TITLE	ABBREVIATION
The Works of John Ruskin, ed. E. T. Cook and Alexander Wedderburn, 1903–12. The Library Edition.	Ruskin, C. & W.
Memoirs and Correspondence of Coventry Patmore, By Basil Champneys, 1900. Two volumes.	Champneys
Thomas Woolner, R. A. His Life in Letters By Amy Woolner, 1917.	Woolner
Greatham Library. Humphrey's Homestead, Greatham, Pulborough, Sussex.	Greatham Library
John J. Burns Library, Boston College Mass. U.S.A. Special Collections.	Boston College

INTRODUCTION

1. The text of this 1923 edition, containing Books I and II only, is reproduced as Appendix A on p. 104. This was the last edition to be published individually and not as part of any collected works. During his lifetime Coventry Patmore revised the text continually.
2. *Daily Telegraph*, 24th July, 1923.
3. This essay, on page 149, is based on a speech Virginia Woolf gave in January, 1931, to the London National Society for Women's Service.
4. Oxford University Press, 1986, p. 291.

CHAPTER ONE

1. *Annual Register*, 1862, p. 204.
2. *Victories Of Love*, 'Letter XI'.

CHAPTER TWO

1. *Evangelical Magazine*, 1818, p. 79.
2. Ruskin, C. & W. Vol. 35, p. 132, *Praeterita* VII.

3. *Sermons* delivered at Beresford Chapel, Walworth, by Edward Andrews, LL.D., 1827. Southwark Council Local Studies Library, S.C. 252, p. 121.

4. *Notes and Queries*, 10th April, 1858.

5. *The Spiritual Times*, Vol. I., p. 56.

6. Ibid, p. 6.

7. Ibid. p. 319.

8. *The Ruskin Family Letters*, Ed. Van Akin Burd, Cornell University Press, 1973, Vol. I., p. 242.

9. *The Ruskin Family Letters*, Vol. I., p. 200.

10. Ruskin, C. & W. Vol. 36, p. 3.

11. *The Ruskin Family Letters*, Vol. I, p. 203.

12. *Through Fifty Years*, The Rev. G. W. Keesey (1891).

13. Andrews Family archives, Australia (Mrs Rennie).

14. Andrews Family archives, England (Miss Bastian).

CHAPTER THREE

1. *Some Account of the Worshipful Company of Clockmakers of the City of London*, S. E. Atkins and W. H. Overall, privately printed, 1881, p. 135.

2. *My Friends and Acquaintance*, Vol. III., p. 50, (1854).

3. The first of these was in January, 1818; the last in June, 1820.

4. These reports appeared in the issues of February, March, and April, 1818.

5. Under the heading 'NOTICES', on an un-numbered page between 610 and 613 of No. XII, Vol. II, March, 1818.

6. The Blackwood Papers, the National Library of Scotland. MS. 4003, f. 200. Letter dated, London 16th April, 1818.

7. The Blackwood papers, MS.ACC. 5643/B1. pp. 42. Letter dated, Edinburgh 19th April, 1818.

8. April, 1818, p. 75.

9. August, 1818, p. 550.

10. Champneys, Vol. II., p. 441, 27th August, 1818.

11. The Blackwood Papers, MS. 1706, f. 104.

12. *London Magazine*, Vol. III, January, 1821, p. 77.

13. The Blackwood Papers, MS. 1706, f. 107.

14. Abraham Bosquett, *A Treatise on Duelling*, London, 1818, p. 87.

15. Andrew Steinmetz, *The Romance of Duelling*, London, 1868. Vol. I., p. 114.

16. Champneys, Vol. I., p. 12.

17. *The Life of Mary Russell Mitford*, Ed. L'Estrange. Vol. II: M.R.M. to Sir William Elford, 22nd March, 1821.

18. *Liber Amoris*, Letter IX. Michael Neve's edition, Hogarth Press, 1985.

19. Vol. XIII, 1823, p. 646.

20. 16th June, 1823.

21. Marriage Register, St George's, Hanover Square, London. 30th August, 1822. The marriage was also announced in *The Scotsman* on 7th September.

22. 1st July, 1854.

23. 23rd July, 1854.

24. *Memoirs of . . . Hazlitt*, Ed. W. Carew Hazlitt. Vol. II., 1867, pp. 247/8.

CHAPTER FOUR

1. Champneys, Vol. I., p. 3.

2. *My Friends and Acquaintance*. P. G. Patmore. Vol. I., p. 209.

3. *My Friends and Acquaintance*, Vol. II., p. 238.

4. The Houghton Collection, Trinity College, Cambridge, letter dated 'Sunday, '44.'

5. Typescript copy of MS letter, dated 11th April, 1846. The Greatham Library.

6. Typed copy of MSS. letter. The Greatham Library. Bulwer Lytton's letter to Coventry is on pp. 54–57 of Champneys, Vol. I., dated Malvern, 27th July, 1844. The original is in the Bodleian Library, Oxford, MS. Eng. misc. c. 107, 10–12.

7. *Punch*, Vol. VII, 1844, p. 4.

8. *English Review*, Vol. IV., October/December, 1845.

9. Letters of *Elizabeth Barrett to Mary Russell Mitford*, Ed. Raymond and Sullivan, Vol. II. Letter No. 348. Baylor University Press, 1983.

10. *Robert Browning and Alfred Domett*, Ed. F. G. Kenyon, p. 107, 1906.

11. The Houghton Collection, Trinity College Cambridge. Letter dated 7th November, 1844.

12. 21st April, 1846.

13. *William Hazlitt*, Augustine Birrell, p. 164.

14. Archives of the British Museum. Minutes of the Trustees' Standing Committee, p. 7074.

15. *Victorians All*, Flora Masson, 1931.

16. *D. G. Rossetti – Family Letters*, Ed. W. M. Rossetti. Vol. II., p. 119. Boston, Roberts Brothers, 1895.

17. *The Betrothal*, 'Idyll XII'.

18. Register of Marriages, entry No. 341. Photographs of their portraits are still to be seen in the vestry, that of Coventry by Brett and of Emily by Millais.

19. *The Espousals*, 'Idyll XII'.

20. *Sussex (Weekly) Advertiser*, 21st September, 1847, p. 7. c.

CHAPTER FIVE

1. Champneys, Vol. II., p. 232.

2. 1st June, 1851.

3. Woolner, p. 7.

4. MS. letter dated 28th October, 1850, Department of Manuscripts, University of Nottingham.

5. Bodleian Library, Oxford. MS. Eng. Litt. d. 293, Item 59.

6. Typescript copy of MS. letter dated 11th April, 1846. Greatham Library.

7. MS. letter dated 14th October, 1851. Houghton Collection, Trinity College, Cambridge.

8. MS. letter, ibid.

9. *William Allingham's Diary*, Ed. G. Grigson, Centaur Press, 1967. Entry for 18th August, 1849.

10. MS. Note, Boston College.

11. Entry for 28th June, 1851.

12. Bodleian Library, Oxford. MS. Facs. d. 278.

13. The Harry Ransom Humanities Research Center, University of Texas. MS. letter, dated 21st August, 1857.

14. Champneys, Vol. II., p. 178.

15. Champneys, Vol. I., p. 138.

16. Pages 67–69.

17. Letter from John Brett to F. G. Stephens, 1st December, 1896. Bodleian Library. MS. Don. e. 81, fols 110–111.

18. Fitzwilliam Museum archives, ref: 245–1920.

19. Brett family archives. (Dr Martin Brett.)

20. *The Espousals*, 'Idyll VI'. Brett quoted here from the Third Edition, 1860. In the First Edition, Coventry wrote, In masses dim, blue hyacinths droop'd, And breadths of primrose cool'd the air.

21. Journal entry, 14th September, 1853.

22. Champneys, Vol. I. pp. 137 & 197.

23. Champneys, Vol. I. p. 209.

24. MS. letter from Richard Garnett to his brother, William John, dated 24th July, 1862. British Library, Dept. of MSS., Ad. MSS. 37,489. f. 354.

25. Champneys, Vol. I., p. 136.

26. Ibid, p. 137.

27. Ibid, p. 139.

28. Ibid, p. 140.

29. Ibid, p. 139.

30. Ibid, p. 137.

31. Ibid, p. 132.

32. Ibid, p. 135.

33. 'Falling in Love', an article in the *Saturday Review* 2nd July, 1870. Coventry Patmore thought that Richard Garnett might have been the author. See letter from Coventry Patmore to Mrs Garnett, 11th July, 1870. Harry Ransom Humanities Research Center, University of Texas.

CHAPTER SIX

1. *Thoughts on Self-Culture, addressed to Women*, by Maria G. Grey and her Sister, Emily Shirreff, 1850. *Women in the Nineteenth Century*, by S. Margaret Fuller, 1850.

2. *The Times*, 14th February, 1851, p. 2.a. The Lords' *Journal*, Vol. LXXXIII, 1851. 13th February, p. 23.a.

3. July, 1851.

4. *The Home Circle*, 18th October, 1851.

5. *Woman's Mission*, Sarah Lewis, 1839.

13th Edn., 1849, reviewed in *The Westminster Review*, Vol. LII., 1850.

  6. *Victories of Love*, 'Letter XI'.

  7. *The Betrothal*. Prologue.

  8. *The Betrothal*, Epilogue.

CHAPTER SEVEN

  1. *The Betrothal*, 'Idyll I'.

  2. Ibid, 'Idyll VI'.

  3. Ibid, 'Idyll VIII'.

  4. Ibid, 'Idyll XII'.

  5. 11th November, 1854, p. 970.

  6. 20th January, 1855.

  7. *The Betrothal*, 'Section IV'.

  8. Champneys, Vol. I., p. 155.

  9. Boston College.

  10. Champneys, Vol. I., p. 165.

  11. MS. Letter at the Ruskin Galleries, Bembridge School, Isle of Wight.

  12. Ibid, dated 19th November.

  13. Trinity College, Cambridge, Houghton Collection, MS. letter, dated 23rd December, 1854.

  14. Ibid, dated 30th January, 1855.

  15. Boston College.

  16. MS. Letter, dated 5th December, 1854. Troxell Collection, The Library, Princeton University, U.S.A.

  17. Boston College. MS. Letter, dated 15th January, 1858.

  18. Woolner, pp. 145 & 147.

  19. MS. letter dated 4th February, 1855. British Library, Dept. of MSS, AD.MSS. 37,489. f. 53.

  20. MS. letter dated 25th April (1858). British Library, Dept. of MSS. AD.MSS. 37,489. f. 187.

  21. As quoted on p. 40, *Richard Garnett* by Barbara McCrimmon. American Library Association, 1989.

  22. 20th October, 1860, p. 479.

  23. Trinity College, Cambridge, Houghton Collection. MS. letter, dated 26th March.

CHAPTER EIGHT

  1. MS. Letter (Photocopy) dated, 5th February, 1857. Bodleian Library, Oxford, MS. Facs. d. 273.

  2. Champneys, Vol. I, p. 133.

  3. Andrews family archives, Australia, (Mrs Rennie). Undated MS. letter. The envelope inscribed, 'Received August 22nd, 1856.'

  4. Boston College. Undated MS. letter.

  5. Ibid.

  6. Ibid.

  7. Ibid.

  8. British Library, Dept. of MSS. AD.MSS. 46125. f. 123. This MS is marked 'Copy of our mother's last letter to Mrs Gemmer. Written a month and a day before she died.'

  9. Typescript copy of MS. letter, dated 17th November, 1861, Greatham Library.

  10. Ibid, 11th March, 1862.

  11. MS. Letter, dated 26th March. Trinity College Library, Cambridge.

  12. Typescript copy of MS letter, dated 12th April, 1862. Greatham Library.

  13. Champneys, Vol. I., p. 151.

  14. *Florilegium Amantis*, 1879.

  15. Champneys. Vol. II., p. 53.

  16. Death certificate, Registration District of Hampstead. 'Cause of death, pulmonary consumption, about 3 years. Convulsions, 2 days.'

CHAPTER NINE

  1. Typed copy of MS. Letter, Greatham Library.

  2. MS. Letter, dated 2nd July. Princeton University Library, U.S.A.

  3. MS. Letter, dated 1st March, 1863. Brett family archives (Mrs Oliver).

  4. Andrews family archives, Australia (Mrs Rennie). Marianne Byle's fortune was £60,000.

  5. First published in *The Pall Mall Gazette* in November, 1876.

  6. Ruskin, C. & W. Vol. 18, p. 120.

  7. Ibid. Vol. 17, p. 362.

  8. *Macmillan's Magazine*, September, 1863, p. 399.

  9. *Frazer's Magazine*, July, 1863, p. 133.

  10. Champneys, Vol. II., p. 238.

  11. Page 5.

  12. *Punch*, 14th June, 1884, p. 279.

13. Written in 1859; published in 1880.
14. Champneys, Vol. II., p. 239.
15. Ibid., p. 216.
16. Typed copy of MS. Letter, dated 5th May, 1887. Greatham Library.
17. Ibid, 20th September, 1887.
18. Champneys, Vol. II., p. 398.
19. 27th November, 1896, p. 10.a.
20. December, 1896, p. 745.
21. Woolner, pp. 331–2.
22. Champneys, Vol. I., p. 344.
23. 28th November, 1896.
24. 5th December, 1896.
25. *Punch*, 5th December, 1896.

Bibliography

There is a comprehensive bibliography of books and articles by and about Coventry Patmore in *The Mind and Art of Coventry Patmore*, by J. C. Reid, Routledge & Kegan Paul, London, 1957. Otherwise, the following books have been consulted over and above those listed in the Source Notes. They have been published in London unless another place is stated.

ON DR ANDREWS AND THE BERESFORD CHAPEL

Edward E. Cleal, *Congregationalism in Surrey*, 1908
Richard W. Mould, *Southwark Men of Mark*, 1905
Edwin Paxton Hood, *The Lamps of the Temple*, 1856
Obituary and Portrait, *The Gospel Magazine*, December, 1841

ON SCOTT'S DUEL WITH CHRISTIE

James P. Gilchrist, *A Chronological Register of The Principal Duels...*, 1821
A Late Captain in the Army, *General Rules and Instructions for all Seconds in Duels*, Dublin, 1801
Horatio Smith, *New Monthly Magazine*, Vol. 81, 1847, 'A Graybeard's Gossip...'
Andrew Lang, *The Life and Letters of John Gibson Lockhart*, 1897
Annual Register, 'Chronicle', February, 1821
St. James's Chronicle, 17th–20th February 1821
The London Chronicle, 19th February 1821
T. J. Barratt, *The Annals of Hampstead*, 1912

FEMINISM AND THE CULT OF HOME

John Killham, *Tennyson and 'THE PRINCESS'. Reflections of an Age*, 1958
Janet Dunbar, *The Early Victorian Woman*, 1953

Deborah Gorham, *The Victorian Girl and the Feminine Ideal*, 1982
G. P. Gilman, THE HOME, *its work and influence*, 1904
H. V. Routh, *Money, Morals and Manners as revealed in Modern Literature*, 1935
Emanuel Swedenborg, *Conjugal Love and its chaste delights*; also, *Adulterous Love and its insane pleasures*, 1768. (English Translation of 1855)
Thomas H. Huxley, *Science and Education*, 1910
John Stuart Mill, *Dissertations and Discussions*, 1867
Chambers's Journal of Popular Literature, 2nd May, 1857: 'A woman's thoughts about women.'
The Saturday Review, 6th August, 1870: 'Womanliness'.
Fraser's Magazine, June, 1840: 'Woman and the Social System.'

THE PRE-RAPHAELITES

The Germ (1850), with An Introduction by W. M. Rossetti (1899), republished by AMS Press, New York, 1965.
W. E. Fredeman (Ed.), *The P. R. B. Journal. William Michael Rossetti's Diary of the Pre-Raphaelite Brotherhood*, O.U.P., 1975.
J. G. Millais, *The Life and Letters of Sir John Everett Millais*, 1899.

For nineteenth-century social history generally, no better source can be found than *The Victorian Frame of Mind, 1830–1870*, by Walter E. Houghton, Yale University Press, 1957, with its extensive bibliography.

Acknowledgements

I thank formally the following authorities for their generous permission to use or quote from documents in their possession. The Trustees of the British Museum; The British Library; The Trustees of the National Library of Scotland; The Master and Fellows of Trinity College, Cambridge; The Syndics of the Fitzwilliam Museum, Cambridge; The Bodleian Library, University of Oxford; The University of Nottingham; The Ruskin Galleries, Bembridge School, Isle of Wight; The Managing Director, Pillans & Wilson, Printers, Edinburgh; The John J. Burns Library, Boston College; The Harry Ransom Humanities Research Center, The University of Texas at Austin; The Trustees of Princeton University, publication with permission of Princeton University Library.

Many people individually, and the librarians and staffs of many institutions collectively, have helped me with this book. I thank them all most sincerely: the descendants of Coventry Patmore and Emily Andrews, his first wife, the 'Angel' - The late Michael Patmore, Mrs Barbara Rennie, Mrs Jenny Young, Mrs Helena Wayne, Miss Julia Bastian; the descendants of John Brett, A.R.A., diarist, and friend of Coventry and Emily Patmore - Dr Martin Brett, Mrs Susan Oliver, Mrs Phyllis Hickox, Mr Michael Hickox; the descendant of Dr Richard Garnett, Coventry Patmore's colleague in the British Museum - Mr Richard Garnett.

I must thank the librarians and staffs of - Boston College, Massachusetts; Princeton University, New Jersey; The University of Texas at Austin; The University of Oxford; The University of Cambridge; The University of Nottingham; The British Library, Great Russell Street; The British Library, Newspaper Library, Colindale Avenue; The British Museum (Archives); The National Library of Scotland; The National Portrait Gallery Library; The City of London, Guildhall Library; The Royal County of Berkshire Library, Reading; The Derbyshire County Library, Derby; The Swiss Cottage Library, Camden; The Barnet Borough Library, Hendon; The Minet Library, Lambeth; The Southwark Local Studies Library; The London Library; The Evangelical Library; Dr Williams' Library; The Greatham Library, Sussex; The

Hastings Museum, Sussex; The Ruskin Galleries, Isle of Wight; The Fitzwilliam Museum, Cambridge; Trinity College, Cambridge.

In particular, especially, I thank Mrs Mary Patmore, widow of Michael Patmore and Mrs Perpetua Ingram, God-daughter of the 3rd Mrs Coventry Patmore; Dr Peter Searby, Fellow of Fitzwilliam College, Cambridge, who read my typescript in draft, and kindly corrected it; Mrs Patricia Aske who compiled a *variorum* of the manuscript of *The Angel* against the First Edition (to be published separately); Mrs Jean Wyllie who researched the Robertson family, Coventry Patmore's maternal ancestors; Mr Stephen Humphrey, Editor of the *Blue Guides* to the Churches and Chapels of Northern and Southern England, whose patience in answering my queries about Dr Andrews and The Beresford Chapel has been monumental; Mrs Barbara Copeland, my Secretary, who, as usual, has prepared everything impeccably; and Sebastian, my son, who has helped me at every stage, with a wide literary knowledge and understanding.

Though every care has been taken to trace the present owners, if inadvertently I have included any copyright material without acknowledgement or permission, I offer my apologies to all concerned.

Index

Compiled by Barbara Hird